How to
Become a
Straight-
Student

D0059296

Also by Cal Newport

How to Win at College

How to Be A High School Superstar

So Good They Can't Ignore You

Deep Work

Digital Minimalism

How to Become a Straight-A Student

The Unconventional
Strategies Real College
Students Use to Score High
While Studying Less

Cal Newport

THREE RIVERS PRESS
NEW YORK

Published in the United States by Three Rivers Press, an imprint of the
Crown Publishing Group, a division of Random House, Inc., New York.
www.crownpublishing.com

THREE RIVERS PRESS and the Tugboat design are registered trademarks of
Random House, Inc.

Originally published in the United States by Broadway Books, an imprint of the
Crown Publishing Group, a division of Random House, Inc., New York, in 2007.

Book design by rlf design

Library of Congress Cataloging-in-Publication Data
    Newport, Cal.
    How to become a straight-A student : the unconventional
    strategies real college students use to score high while studying
    less / Cal Newport. — 1st ed.
        p. cm.
    Includes bibliographical references.
    ISBN-13: 978-0-7679-2271-5
    1. Study skills.   2. College student orientation—United States.
    I. Title.
    LB2395.N515 2007
    378.1'70281—dc22

                                                    2006016081

PRINTED IN THE UNITED STATES OF AMERICA

30 29 28 27

Contents

Introduction 1

Part 1. Study Basics 11

Part 2. Quizzes and Exams 59

Part 3. Essays and Papers 141

Introduction

"My friends always wondered why I was
never in the library, but instead in the student
center socializing, or at a party, or at an
event. They said I made it 'all look so easy.'"

Anna, *a straight-A college student*

This is not your average college study guide. Unlike the titles next to it on the shelf, none of the advice presented here was devised by professors or self-proclaimed academic skills experts. I promise that you won't find any mention of the Cornell note-taking method, mental map diagrams, or any other "optimal learning technique" crafted in an office or laboratory—environments far removed from the realities of typical college life.

Instead, this book reveals—for the first time—the study habits used by real straight-A college students. All of the advice that follows was distilled from a series of interviews I conducted with a large group of top-scoring undergraduates. These participants were drawn predominantly from the Phi Beta Kappa rolls of some of the country's most rigorous colleges and universities—including Harvard, Princeton, Yale, Dartmouth, Brown, Columbia, Duke, Amherst, and Skidmore—and they were carefully chosen to represent a wide variety of academic concentrations. In each interview, I asked the student to detail his or her study habits. The questions ranged from the general ("How do you defeat the urge to procrastinate?") to the specific ("What techniques or systems do you use to locate and organize sources for a research paper?"). If the questionnaire revealed the student to be a grind—someone who earns high grades simply by studying an excessive amount—I discarded the responses. I was interested only in students who improved their grades through smarter, more efficient study skills—not through longer hours and more painful study sessions.

How did I know such students existed? *I am one of them.* When I arrived as a freshman at Dartmouth College, I had no idea how to prepare for exams or write college-level papers. Like most students, I left high school believing that to study meant to reread your class notes and assignments as many times as possible and that paper writing required you to sit down in front of your computer and start typing until you finished. The problem, however, is that college is not high school. The material to be mastered is much more complicated and the professors have higher expectations. In the college environment, simple brute force study methods can end up requiring a lot of time and causing a lot of pain. Nevertheless, most students still rely on them. And this is why they find themselves regularly pulling all-nighters and developing an antagonistic attitude toward their courses. The taxing effects and spotty success of these methods also underlie the common belief that only geniuses and grinds can score top grades.

When I first entered college, I shared in these beliefs. But soon I became dubious. It didn't take long for me to decide that there had to be a better way to learn the material. The results of my studying using simple techniques varied widely—I'd spend all night hacking away at an essay and end up scoring a B-, or give what I thought was a frantic last-minute review for a quiz and score an A. I constantly felt like I was behind in my reading, and there always seemed to be new deadlines on the horizon that I had to scramble to meet. It was truly a chaotic existence. But when I looked around, all of my friends seemed to be having the same experience—and none of them seemed willing to question it. This didn't sit right with me. I wasn't content to work in long, painful stretches and then earn only slightly above-average grades for my efforts. I wanted to be exceptional. And I wanted to achieve this without having to sacrifice sleep or my social life. To many students, such a goal may sound hopelessly hubristic. But I'm an optimist by nature, and, observing the sorry state of my current study skills, I was convinced that I could do better.

It took me most of my freshman year to construct, through repeated experimentation, a toolbox of sufficiently improved study habits. But once I had perfected them, the results were profound. Of the thirty-six courses I took between my sophomore and senior years of college, I scored exactly one A- and 26 perfect As. The most stunning piece of this transformation, however, was how much less time I had to spend on studying. As my strategies became more refined, the hours required were reduced. By my senior year it got to the point where, during finals periods, I would sometimes *pretend* to be heading off to the library just so I wouldn't demoralize my roommates, who were preparing for yet another grim all-nighter.

What was my secret? *Efficiency*. The simple truth is that the brute force techniques used by most students are incredibly inefficient. When it comes to exam preparation, passive review is not an effective way to learn complicated concepts. It's also mentally draining, which further diminishes the rate at which you can absorb and internalize information. For paper writing, this same problem holds. When you approach the task without proper preparation, it becomes incredibly tiring and you can end up spinning your wheels. After a while, even the formation of coherent sentences becomes difficult and time intensive. In contrast, the techniques I came up with were so streamlined that I could learn more material than my classmates and actually spend less time studying. By eliminating stupid habits and wasted effort, I transformed exam prep and paper writing from a dreaded chore to a targeted activity.

For a while, I was convinced that I was unique for having discovered such a smart approach to learning. But, alas, this illusion was soon shattered. It occurred during the winter of my senior year, when I was attending a ceremony celebrating my induction, along with thirty other classmates, into Phi Beta Kappa. This group represented, more or less, the thirty students with the highest G.P.A.s out of my class of over a thousand. Accordingly, I had arrived at the venue prepared to spend the evening with some serious nerds. As it turns out, however, I was in for a surprise.

Upon walking through the door that night, I was immediately struck by how many of the other students I knew socially. These were people who, given their level of visibility on campus, I never would have imagined were scoring straight As. They were magazine editors, frat boys, and crunchy environmentalists. I knew them from parties and campus clubs and through mutual friends. They were, for the most part, normal, well-rounded, and interesting—not at all the type of super-grind one might assume would occupy such an elite level of academic achievement. The lesson of that night was obvious: Perhaps I was not, in fact, as unique as I had first imagined. Maybe there were others out there who had discovered similar secrets to academic success.

The writer instincts in me soon took over. Fascinated to know exactly how these seemingly normal students had done so well, I sent all of my fellow Phi Beta Kappas a survey about their study habits. Most were happy to share their methods and I quickly confirmed that my suspicions were true. Not only were many of them using innovative, homegrown study strategies, but many of these strategies were surprisingly similar to those that I had developed during the previous few years.

At the time I had just finished editing the manuscript for my first book, *How to Win at College*, so I wasn't exactly eager to get started right away with another massive writing project. But after seeing these initial survey responses, I knew I had stumbled onto something big. While most college students toil arduously through the study and paper-writing processes, there exists an elite group of undergrads who have discovered unconventional strategies for earning much higher grades in much less time. I wanted to share these secrets with other students, and thus the idea for this book was born. Soon I was sending out more questionnaires to more straight-A students at colleges around the country, until I gathered enough responses, from students with enough different backgrounds and majors, to distill the advice presented in this guide.

In the pages that follow, you will discover the details of these often surprising study strategies. I've included examples and case studies throughout the book to demonstrate how to apply the advice in many different real-life academic situations. You will learn how to:

- Manage your time and deal with the urge to procrastinate.

- Take targeted notes in class.

- Handle reading assignments and problem sets with ease.

- Prepare efficiently for exams.

- Master the art of exam-taking.

- Write incisive critical analysis essays.

- Conduct thorough research.

- Write standout term papers.

Remember, this advice comes from real students and was honed, through trial and error, in real college classrooms. This distinction is important. It's what separates this book from the many existing study guides that sit next to it on the bookstore shelf. As mentioned, most study guides are written either by professors or academic skills experts, many years separated from their own college experience. The result is that the authors of these guides are disconnected from the realities of undergraduate life.

For example, *How to Study*, by college professors Allan Mundsack, James Deese, and Ellin K. Deese, suggests that students wake up at 7 A.M. each morning, go to sleep by 11 P.M. each night, and on many days schedule only a single hour of "recreation," with the rest of the time dedicated to attending class, eating, or working. One gets the feeling that these professors haven't spent much time socializing with students lately. Even their plan for Friday—the biggest party night of the week—has the student working until 10 P.M., taking a one-hour break, then turning in by eleven.

Student Success Secrets, written by Eric Jensen, a learning expert and professional public speaker, offers equally out-of-touch suggestions. His tips to help you remember concepts learned from a reading assignment include "put it in a picture or poster—use intense colors," "act out the material or do a fun role play in your own room," or "create or redo a song; *make a rap*." Just try to imagine a sophisticated liberal arts major attempting to make a rap about her recent reading assignment concerning post-structuralist interpretations of pre-Victorian English literature! (Key question: What word rhymes with "Foucault"?)

The granddaddy of all unrealistic study guides, however, just might be *What Smart Students Know*, by Princeton Review cofounder Adam Robinson. In this best-selling guide, Robinson suggests—and I swear I am not making this up—that students approach a reading assignment as a *twelve-step process!* That's right, twelve separate steps. Before you even crack the actual assignment, Robinson suggests that you jot down questions about the importance of the reading and then take notes on what you know about the topic, what it reminds you of, and what you want to learn. He then asks you, among other things, to read the assignment a total of three separate times, write and then rewrite your notes, represent the information in picture form, construct "question charts," and devise mnemonics to help you memorize the concepts. Needless to say, this approach to a simple reading assignment is humorously unrealistic. I even did a little math. For a typical college-level liberal arts course, a student might be assigned an average of two hundred pages of reading a week. In his book, Robinson provides a one-page sample reading and describes twenty-three different questions that students might ask about it. At this rate of twenty-three questions per page, spending thirty seconds on each query, we would end up spending around forty hours a week (i.e., a full-time job's worth of time) simply completing one of the twelve steps on the reading assignments for just one class. Sounds like a great plan!

These examples highlight the simple truth that the advice in most existing study guides—written by "experts," not students—is often impractical and time consuming. *How to Become a Straight-A Student*, on the other hand, is the first guide based on the experiences of real college students, and it was written to provide an alternative to the other titles on the market. In the pages that follow, you will find homegrown strategies that are compatible with the demands of your day-to-day student life. They may not be as elaborate as the intricate systems devised by the "experts," but they're easy to implement—and they get the job done. Best of all, when you start putting these strategies into practice, you will experience immediate results.

Keep in mind: If you find a piece of advice that doesn't quite fit your needs or circumstances, that's okay. In fact, you should expect this. Each of the students I interviewed for this book had his or her own unique take on the best way to study. Follow their lead and, when stuck, experiment. Replace techniques you don't like with ones that seem better. If these new techniques work, keep them; if they fail, replace them with something else. The key to improving your grades without becoming a grind cannot be found in any single study habit. It is, instead, rooted in the big picture decision to reject rote review once and for all and begin the flexible search for strategies that work better for you.

Above all, remember that college is a multifaceted experience, of which grades are just one of many important pieces. It's my hope that this book will help you painlessly conquer this one piece so you can have more time and energy to explore all of the others—the friends, the unburdened idealism, the heroic beer consumption—that make these four years so rich.

Part 1
Study
Basics

"Go big or go home. Seriously.
Work hard when you work and
you'll have plenty of time
to play hard."

Lydia, a straight-A college student

A common complaint I hear from students is that they never seem to have enough time to finish all of their work. They vent about how many hours they spend—late nights reviewing in the library, weekends sacrificed to paper writing—but no matter how hard they try, there always seems to be something else due. As Matthew, a straight-A student from Brown, explains, it's easy for college students to become "stuck in a state of permanent catch-up." Understandably, these students feel like they have reached their academic limit; they believe that unless they forgo sleep or any semblance of a social life, there are simply not enough hours in the day to stay on top of all their schoolwork.

Let's start by getting one thing clear: This belief is false. The problem here is not the amount of available hours, but rather how each hour is spent. I know this from firsthand experience. While researching this book, I spent time with some of the country's most accomplished students, and I can assure you that no matter how diligent you think you are, there is a Rhodes scholar out there who fits in three times the amount of work and activities you do and probably still manages to party harder than you would ever dare. I don't mean to imply that everyone should aim to become a drunken Rhodes scholar (though it would certainly be fun to try); rather, my point is that a surprising amount of work, relaxation, and socializing can be extracted from a single twelve-hour day. A lack of time, therefore, isn't enough to explain why so many students feel overwhelmed. So what does explain this phenomenon? The answer, as it turns out, has much more to do with *how* we work than what we're trying to accomplish.

As humans, our minds have evolved to prefer short-term tasks such as "run away from that lion" or "eat food." Therefore, when you walk into the library on a Sunday morning with the goal of finishing all of your homework and writing a paper, your brain isn't happy. The idea of spending eight consecutive hours trapped in a study carrel is dispiriting. Plus, it's hard to focus for that long, so pretty soon fatigue will set in, your concentration will wander, and every distraction will suddenly seem impossibly appealing. Before you know it, the day will be over and you'll realize that you haven't accomplished much productive work at all. The next day, new assignments will pile onto those you didn't finish on Sunday, and the tedious process starts all over again.

Jason, a straight-A student from the University of Pennsylvania, uses the term "pseudo-working" to describe this common approach to studying. The pseudo-worker looks and feels like someone who is working hard—he or she spends a long time in the library and is not afraid to push on late into the night—but, because of a lack of focus and concentration, doesn't actually accomplish much. This bad habit is endemic on most college campuses. For example, at Dartmouth there was a section of the main library that was open twenty-four hours a day, and the students I used to see in there late at night huddled in groups, gulping coffee and griping about their hardships, were definitely pseudo-working. The roommate who flips through her chemistry notes on the couch while watching TV is pseudo-working. The guy who brings three meals, a blanket, and six-pack of Red Bull to the study lounge in preparation for an all-day paper-writing marathon is also pseudo-working. By placing themselves in distracting environments and insisting on working in long tedious stretches, these students are crippling their brain's ability to think clearly and efficiently accomplish the task at hand. The result is fatigue headaches and lackluster outcomes.

The bigger problem here is that most students don't even realize that they're pseudo-working. To them pseudo-work *is* work—it's how they've always done it, and it's how all of their friends do it. It never crosses their mind that there might be a better way. Straight-A students, on the other hand, know all about pseudo-work. They fear it, and for good reason. It not only wastes time, but it's also mentally draining. There is just no way to be well-balanced, happy, and academically successful if you're regularly burning through your free hours in long, painful stretches of inefficient studying. The students I interviewed for this book emphasized again and again the importance of avoiding this trap. In fact, when asked what one skill was most important in becoming a non-grind straight-A student, most of them cited the ability to get work done quickly and with a minimum of wasted effort.

So how do these students achieve this goal? A big part of the solution is timing—they gain efficiency by compressing work into focused bursts. To understand the power of this approach, consider the following simple formula:

work accomplished = time spent x intensity of focus

Pseudo-work features a very low intensity of focus. Therefore, to accomplish something by pseudo-working, you need to spend a lot of time. The straight-A approach, on the other hand, maximizes intensity in order to minimize time. For example, let's rank intensity on a scale of 1 to 10 (with 10 being the most intense). Assume it takes ten hours to finish studying for a test by pseudo-working with a low intensity score of 3. According to our formula, this same amount of work can be accomplished in only three one-hour bursts, each with an intensity of 10. The work that took you all day Sunday to complete could instead be finished by studying an hour after breakfast, an hour after lunch, and an hour after dinner—the rest of the day being free for you to relax!

With this formula in mind, you can begin to understand why many straight-A students actually study *less* than their classmates: They replace long, low-intensity stretches of work with a small number of short, high-intensity sessions. Of course, this is not the whole story behind their success; what straight-A students actually do in these short bursts is also crucial—*technique* is just as important as *timing*. Part Two (Quizzes and Exams) and Part Three (Essays and Papers) of this book are dedicated to these technical details. But learning how to follow an efficient schedule, and banishing pseudo-work from your college experience for good, is a crucial first step toward your academic overhaul.

To accomplish this transformation, however, you will need to gain control over your lifestyle—and that's often no small task. For example, you will need to spread out the intense work sessions so that you have time in between to recharge. This requires basic time-management skills. You're also going to have to overcome your urge to procrastinate, because scheduling your work is meaningless if you don't actually work in the time you set aside. This requires self-motivation. Finally, to obtain the highest possible levels of intensity, you need to choose the right locations, times of day, and durations to study. If you aren't careful about how you select these three factors, you can unintentionally sabotage your ability to focus. This requires a smart planning strategy.

Part One will teach you how to satisfy these requirements. It begins with the presentation of a simple time-management system, customized for the busy college lifestyle. Don't be frightened, the system is incredibly lightweight—it's designed to require only five minutes a day of planning and can survive periods of neglect. Part One then continues with a collection of battle-tested strategies to help you fight procrastination. This advice comes straight from the experiences of real students and has been proven to work amid the chaos and distractions of the typical undergraduate lifestyle—it is simple, easy to apply, and surprisingly effective. This part concludes with a discussion of when during the day, where on campus, and for how long to study to maximize your productivity. The students interviewed for this book experimented extensively to find the right answers to these key questions, and, in this final step, I pass these answers on to you.

Together, these basic skills are the foundation upon which all the advice in this book is built. Without them, you'll be unable to implement the specific study techniques described in the parts that follow. Master them, however, and you will experience improvements in all aspects of your life—not just grades. You'll have more free time, you'll get the sleep you crave, you'll party harder, and you'll be able to devote more energy to your extracurricular interests. So relax. You are about to take your first step toward a much more enjoyable and productive college experience.

Step 1

Manage Your Time in Five Minutes a Day

Real straight-A students, like most reasonable students, hate time management. After all, college is supposed to be about intellectual curiosity, making new friends, and becoming obsessed with needlessly complicated drinking games. An overwhelming interest in time management is best left to harried business executives (or, perhaps, premeds). At the same time, however, you can't abandon all attempts to keep tabs on your schedule. As mentioned in the introduction to Part One, all of the techniques described in this book require some ability to control your schedule. Ignore this skill, and you doom yourself to four long years of playing catch-up with your work. As Doris, a straight-A student from Harvard, states: "Time management is critical—it's a skill that you absolutely must develop over the course of your time at college."

Most students, however, misunderstand the purpose of time management—they believe it's used only to cram as much work as possible into the day. But this is not the main motivation behind controlling your schedule. As it turns out, a little planning goes a long way toward reducing your daily stress levels. Having deadlines and obligations floating around in your mind is exhausting—it makes it impossible to completely relax, and, over time, can lead you down the path toward a breakdown. However, once you figure out what work needs to be done and when, it's like a weight being lifted from your shoulders. The uncertainty vanishes: When you work, you can fully concentrate on the assignment in front of you, and when you relax, you can do so without any anxiety. "I don't believe in giving up anything," says Jenna, a straight-A student from Princeton. "Not my social life, not my extracurricular activities, not my academic success." Basic control over your schedule breeds balance. This is why time management, as Doris stated earlier, is the key to getting the most out of all aspects of your college experience.

The goal of Step #1 is to present a time-management system that helps you achieve this stress-free balance without requiring you to sacrifice the spontaneity and excitement of college. Specifically, we present a system tailored to the typical undergraduate lifestyle that meets the following criteria:

1. Requires no more than five to ten minutes of effort in a single twenty-four-hour period.

2. Doesn't force an unchangeable minute-by-minute schedule on your day.

3. Helps you remember, plan, and complete important tasks be-fore the very last moment.

4. Can be quickly restarted after periods of neglect.

We will cover the details of this system in a few simple steps and then conclude with a detailed case study so you can see how it works in a realistic setting.

What You Need

This system requires two pieces of equipment.

1. **A calendar**: It doesn't matter what type of calendar, and it's not something that you have to carry around with you. It can be Microsoft Outlook or iCal on your computer, a cheap day planner, or one of those advertisement-laden freebies they hand out at orientation. It just has to be something that you can reference every morning that has enough space to record *at least a dozen items* for each day.

2. **A list:** Some piece of writing material that you can update throughout the day. This you *do* have to carry around with you, so make it something simple, like a sheet of paper ripped out of a notebook each morning.

The Basic Idea

Record all of your to-dos and deadlines on your calendar. This be-comes your master schedule, the one place that stores everything you need to do. The key to our system, however, is that you need to deal with your calendar only once every twenty-four hours. Each morning, you look at it to figure out what you should try to finish that day. Then, throughout the day, whenever you encounter a new to-do or deadline, simply jot it down on your list. The next morning, you can transfer this new stuff from your list onto your calendar, where it's safe. And we're back where we started.

That's it. Pretty simple, right? The whole system can be summarized in three easy steps: (1) Jot down new tasks and assignments on your list during the day; (2) next morning, transfer these new items from your list onto your calendar; and (3) then take a couple of minutes to plan your day.

Now, we'll examine these steps in a little more detail. In particular, we need some strategies for how to plan your day each morning using your calendar and what to do when unexpected events interfere and turn that plan upside down (trust me, this will happen more often than not).

Update Your Calendar Each Morning

This is where the magic happens. Every morning, spend a few minutes to update your calendar and figure out what you should try to accomplish. This is the only serious time-management thinking you have to do for the whole day, so the demand is pretty reasonable. This updating process should proceed as follows:

Find your list from the day before. It will probably look something like the example described in Figure 1. Don't worry too much about how this list is formatted; we will discuss that shortly. For now, focus

Figure 1. Sample List

Tuesday—1/24/06

Today's Schedule	Things to Remember
• ~~10:00 to 12:00 Econ class~~	
• ~~12:00 to 1:00 Lunch with Rob~~	• Econ study group, Thur. at 9 P.M.
• ~~1:00 to 1:45 Government reading~~	• French quiz moved to Friday.
• ~~2:00 to 4:00 Government class~~	
• ~~4:00 to 5:30 Finish government reading~~	• Laundry
• 5:30 to 6:30 Start French essay	• Start researching summer internship opportunities.

on the "things to remember" column, which contains the new to-dos and deadlines that were jotted down throughout the day.

Transfer these new items onto your calendar. Write the deadlines on the appropriate dates, and write the to-dos on the days when you plan to complete them. Following the example of our sample list, you would first jot down the econ study group time under Thursday's date and the French quiz under Friday's date. You would then choose a day to do laundry and jot down a reminder under that date, and choose a day to start internship research and jot down a reminder under this date. You can move these items around on your calendar as many times as you want, so don't worry too much about which date you initially choose for a new to-do. However, try to use some common sense. For example, if Wednesday afternoon and evening are packed with meetings and work, this might not be the best day to schedule doing your laundry. Similarly, if you have a big test Monday morning, don't schedule a lot of annoying errands for Sunday;

you'll need your concentration for studying. If something is not especially time sensitive, such as the internship research example from above, don't be afraid to put it on a day far in the future, at a point when you know you will be less busy—such as right after midterms or at the beginning of a new semester.

Next, move the to-dos that you planned for yesterday, but didn't complete, to new days on your calendar. In our sample list from Figure 1, the Today's Schedule column describes to-dos planned from the day before. As you can see, in this example, all the to-dos were completed except the "Start French essay" task, so you would need to move this task to a new date.

At this point, your calendar once again holds everything that you need to get done. Now it's time to figure out your plan for the current day. Go ahead and trash yesterday's list—it's served its purpose—and grab a fresh sheet of paper to use as today's list. Divide it into two columns, as shown in Figure 1, and label them *Today's Schedule* and *Things to Remember*, respectively.

Next, look at the calendar entry for the current day. It will probably contain a handful of appointments and to-dos. Your goal is to figure out how much of this work you can realistically accomplish. You might be tempted to simply copy all of these tasks into your Today's Schedule column and then treat it as a simple to-do list for the day. *Don't do this!* If you want to avoid getting overwhelmed by your work, you need to be smarter about your time.

Here is what you should do instead: **Try to label each of your to-dos for the day with a specific time period during which you are going to complete it.** Be honest. Don't record that you are going to study for three hours starting at three if you know that you have a meeting at five. And be reasonable about how long things really take—don't plan to read two hundred pages in one hour. For simplicity, group many little tasks (errands that take less than ten minutes) into one big block (for example: *"10:00 to 10:45—mail letter, return library book, buy new deodorant, fill out transcript request form at registrar"*). Leave plenty of time for breaks. Give yourself an hour for meals, not twenty minutes. And, if possible, end your day at an appropriate hour; don't try to fit in work right up until sleep time because you need to be able to unwind and relax. In general—though it may seem counterintuitive—be pessimistic. The truth is: Things will come up. Don't assume that every hour that looks free in the morning will stay free throughout the day.

Remember, the goal here is not to squeeze everything into one day at all costs, but rather to find out how many of the tasks listed for the day you actually have time to accomplish. If you can't fit all the to-dos into your schedule for the day, no problem! Simply move the remaining items onto the calendar entries for future dates. You can deal with them later.

Your final step is to record the tasks you will have time for into the Today's Schedule column of your list. As shown in Figure 1, label each task with its time. That's it. You can now reference your list throughout the day to remind yourself of what you should be doing and when.

But here's the important point: The specific times on your schedule aren't set in stone—they're more of a suggestion. As we will discuss shortly, you will be free to move tasks around throughout the day, depending on your energy level and unexpected events that may arise. The main reason you break down your to-dos into time slots is to help you avoid the common student mistake of overestimating your free time. Many well-intentioned students use a simple to-do list to keep track of their daily obligations. But without time labeling, they have no idea how much they can actually accomplish, leading to an unrealistic plan. A twelve-hour day seems like a large amount of time, but when you account for meals and classes and meetings and breaks and socializing, your schedule suddenly becomes a lot tighter. The equation is simple: If you overestimate your free time, then you are likely to put off work until it's too late. And this leads to all-nighters, panic attacks, and shoddy performance. A realistic sense of time is arguably one of the most important factors in succeeding as a student. After a week or two of time labeling your to-dos, you will be well along your way toward developing this crucial trait.

Use the List During the Day

As you move through your day, use the rough schedule recorded under the Today's Schedule column to remind yourself what you should be doing. Keep in mind that the student lifestyle is, generally, quite unpredictable. Things will always come up at the last minute. Work will take longer than expected, your roommate will point you toward some absurd Web site that immediately demands an afternoon of your scrutiny—you know how it goes. So adjust your time labels as many times as needed. But don't procrastinate excessively! The list you constructed in the morning should contain a reasonable amount of work, so if your schedule doesn't become too unexpectedly crazy, you should be able to accomplish most, if not all, of these tasks. In general, if you're completing most of what's on your list at least five days out of seven, then you're as productive as any student realistically needs to be. If not, don't worry—the next section of Part One will teach you how to combat your urge to procrastinate.

Remember, your list also serves another important purpose. During the day you will probably encounter various *new* to-dos and deadlines that need to be scheduled. For example, a professor might announce the date of an upcoming exam, or a friend might give you the date and time for an upcoming study group. The key is to get these obligations out of your head as soon as possible so your mind is not unnecessarily cluttered. Jot down a quick reminder on your list, in the Things to Remember column, as soon as they occur. This takes only a few seconds, and then you can forget about them. The actual scheduling of these tasks will take place the next morning; all you have to do for now is scribble a few words on a piece of scrap paper.

Remember, to-dos and deadlines that exist only in your mind drain your energy, distract your attention, create stress, and are more likely to be forgotten. When you're working, you should be able to concentrate on working, and when you're relaxing, you should be able to enjoy relaxing. But you can't devote 100 percent of your energy to any activity when you have important reminders bouncing around in your head.

Few students have the energy to schedule every new piece of information that comes along during the day. Think about this for a moment: If it's the middle of the afternoon, and you are hungry, and everyone is just getting up to leave at the end of a long class, when suddenly the professor yells out a notice that a paper topic is due the following week... you're probably not going to have the energy to stop packing up, take out a calendar, think about what steps are involved in coming up with a paper topic, and then schedule each step on the appropriate days. It would be nice if you did, because then you could purge the deadline from your mind and be confident that it's safely recorded in your calendar—but this is unrealistic. And it violates our original criterion that any time-management system should require only a few minutes each day.

That's the power of the "things to remember" column of your list. You can't expect yourself to be able to think seriously about time management at all points during your busy day. But the act of pulling out a piece of scrap paper from your pocket and quickly jotting down "anthro paper topic" requires minimal energy, no thinking, and barely any time. You don't have to consider when to begin working on the paper topic, what steps are involved, or how many days it will require. You simply scribble down three words.

The key is that the list is a trusted piece of storage. You are confident that tomorrow morning, when you're doing your only time-management thinking for the day, you will see that reminder and record the appropriate steps in your calendar. Because of your list, the deadline will not be lost. It will be scheduled.

Restarting After a Period of Neglect

To date, I have yet to have successfully followed any time-management system without interruption for longer than two months. I try, but inevitably I hit a rough patch. Typically, this happens during the few days following a really busy period—I'm so exhausted from the intensity of the preceding work that I find myself unable to even mention the word "to-do" without breaking into a cold sweat. This happens to everyone, and you can expect that periodically it will happen to you too. Don't fear these occasions, and don't let them make you feel like a failure. They're normal.

The key point is that these lapses are temporary. After a couple days of swearing off my calendar, I always find myself growing uncomfortable with the increasing number of obligations that are free floating in my mind. Before I know it, I'm back into the swing of using the system again, and no worse for wear. The same will be true for you. Once you have learned the power of feeling organized, you will have a hard time going long periods without it.

Fortunately, the system described here is adaptable to these periods of neglect. If you skip a few days, all you need to do upon restarting is to dump all the to-dos and deadlines free floating in your mind onto a sheet of paper and then push these back onto your calendar for future dates.

Case Study: A Monday with Stephen

Even the simplest systems can come across as confusing when first described. So let's go through a quick example that will show you how to put this system into practice. Stephen's story is based upon the real-life college experiences of myself and the many students I interviewed. If you're already at college, what follows will seem familiar. If you haven't yet started your undergraduate career, don't panic! Yes, Stephen has a lot on his plate. Notice, however, how he uses our system to keep control of his many obligations. Though he can't finish everything in one day, he remains confident that everything that needs to get done will get done in time. As you read this example, imagine how Stephen's stress might increase, and his efficiency decrease, if he didn't have his list and calendar to guide his actions and capture the new to-dos and deadlines that constantly pop up.

Monday Morning

Stephen gets up early because he has class at 9:30 A.M.—a horrible thing. He grabs his calendar from his desk and roots around in his hamper to find the sheet of notebook paper that he used as yesterday's list. He has only a couple of minutes before class, but that's okay. Our system requires very little time.

Figure 2 shows what Stephen finds recorded on his calendar for today.

Figure 2. Stephen's calendar entry for Monday

Monday—3/11/07

- *Finish reading for Tuesday Gov class.*
- *Gift for Dad's birthday*
- *First step of research for Gov paper—find books, Xerox relevant chapters.*
- *Pay cell phone bill.*
- *Return Mark's CD.*
- *First half of Econ problem set (due Wed)*
- *Pick topic for Anthro paper (due tomorrow).*
- *Read five chapters from Anthro book (need to catch up for Friday's quiz).*
- *Dinner with guys—7 P.M.—Molly's*
- *Ill-conceived toga party—10 P.M.—Alpha Chi*

Figure 3. Stephen's list from Sunday

Sunday—3/10/07

Today's Schedule

- ~~1:00 to 3:00—read article for Anthro.~~
- ~~3:00 to 6:00—write Government essay.~~
- ~~7:00 to 8:00—dinner with Sarah~~
- ~~9:00 to 10:00—edit Government essay.~~
- 10:00 to 11:00—start reading for Tuesday's Government class

Things to Remember

- Call home.
- Start researching summer internships.
- Create schedule for practicing guitar?

Figure 3 shows what he finds scrawled on yesterday's list.

There are several things to notice here. First, Stephen has a lot of work recorded on his calendar entry for today. More than he can probably accomplish in twelve hours, so some of these to-dos will need to be moved to other dates. Also notice Stephen's schedule from the day before (Sunday). This is typical. A fun night on Saturday inevitably leads to a late start and a large workload on Sunday. Stephen was too ambitious with his planning, and by 10:00 P.M. he was burnt out from working on his essay and never got around to starting the Government reading he had scheduled. So this task will need to be carried over to today. Finally, notice how Stephen's Things to Remember column from yesterday includes some long-term projects, such as "Create schedule for practicing guitar." This is a great use of the list! If you jot down ideas for extracurricular and personal projects as they occur to you, they will get moved onto your calendar and therefore won't be forgotten until you finally get around to doing something about them.

Now let's see how Stephen gets a handle on all of this before class.

What Does Stephen Do First?

Stephen's first step is to time label the tasks currently on his plate so he can determine how much he can actually get done. Between his calendar entry for today and the leftovers from yesterday's list, Stephen has a *lot* of to-dos to schedule. His strategy is simple: He starts time labeling in order of importance until his schedule is full, and then moves the rest of the items to other days on the calendar. To effectively time label, however, he must first figure out how much free time he has available. Stephen quickly runs through the following in his head:

> *I have class from 9:30 to 10:30, and another class from 11:00 to 12:00. It's unlikely that I will get any work done between my 7:00 P.M. dinner and the Alpha Chi party that starts soon after. I should also try to squeeze in an hour or two for a predinner workout (have to look good in that toga), so I should aim to be done with all of my work by 5:00.*

With his free time now identified, Stephen can begin to time label his to-dos. Here is his thought process:

> *In between class, from 10:30 to 11:00, I can squeeze in my three small tasks—pay cell phone bill, buy a birthday gift for Dad, and return Mark's CD. After my second class, I will need to get lunch, but then I should get right to work on my Government*

*reading because it's due tomorrow! Let's see, I have three Government articles to read, which will realistically take two hours, so I will label this task with **1:00** to **3:00**. Hmmmm, I am running out of time here. I need to start that Econ problem set because those suck, and it's due Wednesday morning, so I'll label that task with **3:00** to **4:30**. Okay, I am down to my final half hour. What else has to get done? My Anthro paper topic is due tomorrow, so I will have to squeeze that in at **4:30** to **5:00**. And that's all I have time for.*

At this point, Stephen is almost done. All that's left is taking care of the still-unscheduled to-dos by moving them to future dates. Remember, these include both the unscheduled tasks recorded for the current day and the "things to remember" items from yesterday's list.

*On yesterday's list I have a reminder to Call home ... this week is so busy ... okay, I'll jot that down on the calendar entry for **Friday**, I'll be more relaxed by then. I really don't have time right now for these other two reminders—start internship research and create guitar schedule—so I'll jot those down on the calendar entry for the **first weekend after midterms** are over. I should have more free time then. Okay, what's left? The unlabeled items from today's calendar entry. No problem. I can move the Anthro reading to **tomorrow's** calendar entry, and then move the Government paper research to **Wednesday**—I can work on it after I hand in my Econ problem set. Done!*

That's it. Stephen has finished all of his serious time-management thinking for the day. Before leaving for class, he rips out a fresh sheet of notebook paper to use for today's list. He divides it into two columns and jots down the tasks he scheduled for the day. Figure 4 shows what Stephen's list looks like as he bolts out the door.

The entire process described above would realistically take only around three to five minutes to complete. The more you use this system, the more natural it becomes. Before you know it, updating your calendar and dashing off a daily schedule will become as routine as taking a morning shower. Remember, this is the only serious time-

Figure 4. Stephen's list on Monday morning

Monday—3/11/07

Today's Schedule	Things to Remember
• 9:30 to 10:30 Class	
• 10:30 to 11:00—Gift for Dad's birthday, pay cell phone bill, return Mark's CD.	
• 11:00 to 12:00—Class	
• 12:00 to 1:00 Lunch/Break	
• 1:00 to 3:00 Do Government reading assignment.	
• 3:00 to 4:30 Start work on Econ problem set.	
• 4:30 to 5:00 Come up with topic for Anthro paper.	
• 5:00 to 7:00 Get huge.	
• 7:00 Dinner followed by inevitable embarrassment at toga party (Note to self: Flex a lot at party.)	

management thinking that Stephen has to do all day. Now he's ready to face his Monday with his mind free from worry about tasks he's forgetting or due dates that are looming. He knows he has scheduled all the tasks on his plate and that they will get done eventually. He has a flexible plan. And he can trust it.

Now let's see how Stephen holds up . . .

During the Day on Monday

The day starts off fine. Stephen successfully finishes the small tasks that he scheduled for **10:30**. During his second class, he remembers that he has some overdue library books that need to be returned. No problem. Stephen whips the list out of his pocket and jots down *"Return books"* under the "Things to Remember" column. A little later, the professor announces the date and time of the midterm—something else that needs to be scheduled. Again, no problem for Stephen. He adds *"Sched. Gov midterm (4/5, 3 P.M.)"* to his list, and then leaves the classroom confident that these tasks will be scheduled appropriately tomorrow morning.

After a leisurely lunch, Stephen hunkers down in the library to tackle his government reading. The articles are a little shorter than usual, so he finishes by **2:30,** which is nice.

As he leaves the library, however, Stephen runs into a friend who convinces him to tag along on a Wal-Mart run. To be honest, it didn't take much convincing. College students, for some inexplicable reason, love Wal-Mart runs.

After this (unavoidable) detour, Stephen gets back to campus by **3:30**. Now he's behind schedule. Quickly checking his e-mail, Stephen sees a message from a classmate asking if he wants to join a study group at 4:00 to work on the Econ problem set. Swiftly adapting,

Stephen once again whips out his list and makes a couple of rapid changes to the Today's Schedule column. He bumps up the Anthro paper topic work to start now, and then replaces his Econ problem set work with the study group that he just found out about. One of the big advantages of this system is its flexibility. Schedules will always change, but this the system makes it easy for you to regain your focus after getting sidetracked. Figure 5 shows the new state of Stephen's list.

Figure 5. Stephen's list Monday afternoon

Monday—3/11/07

Today's Schedule	Things to Remember
• ~~9:30 to 10:30—Class~~	• *return books.*
• ~~10:30 to 11:00—Gift for Dad's birthday, Pay cell phone bill, Return Mark's CD.~~	• *Sched. Gov midterm (4/5, 3 P.M.)*
• ~~11:00 to 12:00—Class~~	
• ~~12:00 to 1:00—Lunch/Break~~	
• ~~1:00 to 3:00—Do Government reading assignment.~~	
• *3:30 to 4:00—Choose Anthro paper topic*	
• *4:00 to 5:00—Work with group on Econ problem set*	
• *5:00 to 7:00—Get huge.*	
• *7:00—Dinner followed by inevitable embarrassment at toga party. (Note to self: Flex a lot at party.)*	

The Anthro work goes fine. Stephen finds a topic that he is happy with and then runs off to meet with his Econ group. During the meeting, the group agrees to meet again Tuesday morning to finish the problem set. Stephen quickly jots down "*Econ group—10 A.M.*" under Things to Remember and then heads off to the gym. He's done with work for the day.

The Aftermath

Because he finished a lot of work during the morning and afternoon before the party, Stephen was able to really relax and have a good time that night. In addition, he successfully recorded all of the new to-dos and deadlines that cropped up during the day. Instead of bouncing around in his head and causing stress, they were safely placed in Stephen's system and will be scheduled in due time. Most important, none of this required him to explicitly think about time management beyond the five minutes he spent planning that morning and the quick rescheduling he did in the afternoon.

As suggested at the beginning of this case study, imagine for a moment what Stephen's day might have been like without the simple time-management system. What if, instead, he'd employed the strategy used by most students and simply tried to remember what he needed to get done? It's highly unlikely that the small tasks—returning a CD, buying a birthday gift, paying a bill—would have been completed. Without a schedule, people don't like to do menial chores unless they're 100 percent necessary. There's also a good chance that he would have forgotten about the Anthro paper topic altogether after the last-minute study group came up.

What about the big-picture reminders from Sunday—calling home, scheduling internships, creating a guitar-practicing schedule?

Those would have been pushed out of his head completely by the demands of near-future deadlines. Without a system to capture them, we can't expect Stephen to remember long-term ideas for any extended period of time.

Most important, without the system, Stephen would have completed much less schoolwork on Monday. The day would have focused, more or less, only on the Government reading, because that was the only big task actually due the next day. Without time labels, Stephen would have had a much hazier understanding of his free time, so he probably wouldn't have started this reading until later in the afternoon (for the most part, students don't like to start any work without a large block of free time ahead of them). Remember, however, that this assignment took a couple of hours to complete, so that means if Stephen had waited until the afternoon to start, he would have finished only this single task by 5:00, with the Econ problem set and Anthro paper topic likely falling by the wayside. Instead, Stephen ended up finishing six tasks by 5:00, leaving plenty of time for exercise and debauchery during the evening.

As you can see from the case study, this simple time-management system, which requires only a few minutes of planning each day, made Stephen significantly more productive and significantly less stressed. It will do the same for you. In other words, five minutes every morning and a sheet of scrap paper in your pocket are enough to transform you from a stressed-out student struggling to get things done, into an organized, relaxed, finely tuned academic machine.

If you remember one lesson from this book, it should be the lesson of this case study: A little organization goes a hell of a long way.

Step 2

Declare War on Procrastination

In the previous section we introduced a simple time-management system to help you plan your day intelligently. That was the easy part. Anyone can spend five minutes to figure out what they *should* be doing. The real challenge is marshaling the motivation to actually do the work once it's scheduled. Without some control over your schedule, you cannot be a happy and successful student—no matter how good your intentions.

As you might expect, in conducting interviews for this book, I put a significant focus on the issue of procrastination. Anyone who makes straight As has clearly found a way to consistently get work done when it needs to be done, and I wanted to find out how. As it turns out, however, I was in for a surprise.

Every student I interviewed was asked the following question:

"How do you defeat procrastination?" As soon as the first responses were returned, it became clear that something was not quite right. I received answers such as:

"I don't."

"Rarely."

"I didn't."

"I don't think that you can."

These were not the responses that I expected—it didn't make sense! Everything else they told me about how they studied and wrote papers clearly indicated that these scholastic studs were kicking some very serious procrastinatory ass, so why were they all claiming they didn't defeat procrastination? What was going on here? Fortunately, many students went on to qualify this first reaction, and it was in these qualifications that I began to figure out what they really meant.

"I don't think that you can," was how Lee, a straight-A student from Columbia, began his answer, but he soon added: "You just have to try to limit it."

Ryan, a straight-A Dartmouth student, started by claiming, "Really, I don't defeat procrastination." But then he continued: "Or, at least, I don't think I do . . . although, I suppose, compared to the majority of students, I'm not as bad as I think."

"I don't know that I've yet defeated procrastination," was how Christine, a straight-A Harvard student, began before concluding: "but I've found ways to make this inevitable tendency less destructive."

Over time, these extended responses began to paint a clear picture. When the straight-A students answered "I don't defeat procrastination," they really meant to say "I don't defeat the *urge* to procrastinate." And this makes perfect sense. To put it simply, some work just plain sucks, and you, like the straight-A students inter-viewed for this book, will want to procrastinate on this sucky work. It's unavoidable. Therefore, the goal in this step is not to teach you how to love all work and never feel like procrastinating ever again. In-stead, I'm going to describe some targeted strategies to help you *sidestep* this unavoidable urge when it arises—not destroy it alto-gether. This is how straight-A students prevent procrastination from destabilizing their schedule. They don't rely only on willpower and good intentions, but instead deploy an arsenal of specific, tested rules that help them short-circuit their natural desire to procrasti-nate. These students, of course, aren't perfect, and they still occasion-ally put off work for no good reason. But overall their strategies made them significantly more effective at following a study plan than their peers—and this made all the difference.

What follows are five anti-procrastination battle plans drawn di-rectly from my straight-A interviews. These techniques are not theo-retical; they are exhaustively used by real students to beat down procrastination again and again. Trust them. Put them into practice immediately. Make them into a habit. The effect will be immediate. You may never fully rid yourself of the urge to procrastinate, and that's okay. But with the right strategies in place, you can rid yourself of the fear that you'll always give in to that urge.

Procrastination Battle Plan #1:
Keep a work progress journal

Think about the last time that you procrastinated on something im-portant. You can probably recall some of the wishy-washy excuses your mind concocted for delaying the work. Something along the lines of "*I don't have all the materials here with me now, but if I waited until tomorrow, I could get started right away with everything I need,*" or "*It's getting late, and my concentration is waning, it would be a waste to start now, so I will wait to tackle this when I'm fresh in the morning.*" Why are these excuses necessary? Why don't we simply think: "*This is boring, and I'm lazy, so I'm not going to do it,*" which is much closer to the truth? The answer is that your ego is a powerful force. We procrastinate, but we don't want to admit to ourselves that we procrastinate. So we make excuses to ourselves to avoid the truth.

A work progress journal is a simple tool that takes advantage of this reality to help you defeat procrastination. It works as follows: Buy a cheap spiral notebook, and keep it near your calendar. Each morning, when you work out your schedule for the day, quickly jot down in the notebook the date and the most important tasks that you are scheduled to get done. At the end of the day, if you've completed all of these tasks, simply jot down *all completed*. If you failed to complete some tasks, record this, along with a quick explanation.

The system adds only an extra minute to your morning routine and requires only an extra minute each night before you go to sleep. It's simple enough to turn into a habit. What's amazing, however, is the journal's immediate effect. Having to record, in ink, on paper, that you procrastinated over a task for no good reason is a powerful blow to your ego. It might be easy to *tell* yourself a few weak excuses for putting off a tedious assignment, but when you have to *record* these same excuses on paper their foolishness is exposed. You can no longer get away with lame rationalizations. This is especially true if you continue to delay the same task day after day. After seeing all of those excuses pile up in your journal, there will be no escape from reality: You are being lazy! Your ego won't like this truth, so it will kick-start your motivation in an effort to avoid it.

The journal, in this way, acts like a personal drill sergeant, sitting on your shoulder and yelling into your ear: "*Soldier, I want you to go get me a pillow, because I know I must be dreaming. I thought I just saw you consider not starting your paper this afternoon, and I knnnoooowwww you wouldn't try to pull that crap with me standing right next to you! Now go grab your notes and get workin' before I make you record your laziness in ink where everyone can see it!*"

Many students, myself included, don't keep a journal all the time, but use it to help them get through unusually busy periods. For example, my work progress journal was a key force in getting me through my senior fall semester, which involved classes, grad school applications, and the writing of my first book. Others have had great success with the journal to keep focused on their LSAT preparation while juggling the demands of regular class work. Some students go so far as to use the system with a friend, agreeing to review each other's journal once a week. As Christine from Harvard suggests: "If you have a friend in the same class, check up on each other's progress." And even if you can't find a willing journal partner, there are other ways to use friends to jump-start your drive: "It helps to simply tell your roommates of your goals, and have them guilt-trip you into working."

Procrastination Battle Plan #2: *Feed the Machine*

Low energy breeds procrastination. Most students know the feeling—your mind starts to feel sluggish, you begin to read whole pages of text without remembering a single word, and writing coherent notes becomes a Herculean task.

It's almost impossible to motivate yourself to stick to a schedule under these mental conditions. Accordingly, during long work periods, you need to feed your body the fuel it needs to perform at its peak. Think of your brain like a machine. If you want to defeat procrastination, you need to provide it with the energy necessary to concentrate and win the fight. Without proper care, it will turn against you.

The nutritional rules for maximizing your mental energy while studying are simple:

1. **Drink water constantly.** Have a water bottle with you, or make frequent trips to the water fountain. One of my favorite study spots had a dispenser of mini–paper cups next to the fountain. My habit was to drink five mini-cups of water every forty-five minutes. It worked wonders toward keeping my mind humming and my energy high. Your body needs water to function. Hydration increases your energy, masks boredom-induced food cravings, and staves off sleepiness. And don't worry about the inevitable side effect of so much drinking. As Greta, a straight-A Dartmouth student, exults: "Frequent bathroom trips keep me awake."

2. **Monitor your caffeine intake carefully.** Don't drink more than one large caffeinated beverage in any one-hour period. While a Coke or cup of coffee can heighten your concentration, too much caffeine in a short period will make you jumpy and un-focused. If you're a coffee drinker, start off with a strong brew

to jump-start your mind, but switch to decaf, tea, or just water for the next hour or two before returning to another strong drink.

3. **Treat food as a source of energy, not satisfaction**. When studying, carefully choose snacks that promise a long-term energy boost. Try vegetables, fruit, anything whole grain, lean proteins, peanuts, or natural granola bars. Refined carbohydrates, such as sugar and white flour, will provide only a quick energy rush followed immediately by a damaging energy drain and increased appetite. Avoid these unhealthy snacks at all costs while working. If you follow rule one, your frequent water consumption will dull the cravings for specific foods, making it much easier to stick with healthier fare.

4. **Don't skip meals.** Snacks alone are not enough to fuel your mind for long periods. Even on the busiest of days, eat regular meals. If you skip breakfast to get a jump start on studying, or put off lunch until the late afternoon so you can finish your reading, you will experience more hunger than your snacks can effectively satisfy. Hunger, and the corresponding low blood sugar, will rob you of your ability to concentrate and set you up to succumb to procrastination. So keep your meals regular. If you're pressed for time, eat fast. Grab a sandwich from a less-populated dining hall and sit alone, or bring part of the meal back to your study location. But never miss meals altogether.

Procrastination Battle Plan #3:
Make an event out of the worst tasks

Some tasks are so horrible that even just the thought of beginning them can send chills down your spine. For me, these included writing personal statements for graduate school applications. Other students cringe at having to type the first few paragraphs of a long paper, composing cover letters for job applications, or beginning the slog through a hopelessly large reading assignment on a hopelessly boring topic (I can't help but remember one particularly descriptive article I had to read about the various clays used in ancient Cypriot vase-making).

It seems to take an extraordinary effort to start these projects before the last possible minute. But it doesn't have to be this difficult. As Laura, a straight-A Dartmouth student, explains: "When studying for something I don't especially enjoy, I try to make an event out of it." Find an out-of-the-way restaurant, coffee shop, or bookstore café. It helps if your location is farther than walking distance from campus. Set a time to bring your work there, and if you don't have a car, arrange to be dropped off and picked up later, or choose a location that takes a while to reach by foot so you won't be tempted to leave right away. Tell everyone you know that you will be gone during this time, and talk up how horrible the work is that you have to complete. The more people who know about your quest, the harder it will be for you to cancel it.

The novelty of the location, plus its distance from campus, will help jump-start your motivation to tackle your horrible task once there.

"I find the change of scenery puts your body in work mode, just as going to the office is supposed to," explains Sean, a straight-A student from Yale. You went through a lot of effort to get to your unusual study nook, and there is no easy way to be distracted. Campus is far away, and therefore so are your friends, your TV, the student center, and your Internet connection. You are sitting alone at a table in a public place, surrounded by strangers, and if you don't start doing something soon, people will begin to wonder: *Who is that odd student sitting alone and staring into space? Is she a drifter? Is she going to snap and kill us all? What's her deal?*

"It's just too awkward to sit there while staring at other people," says Laura, "so inevitably I will end up reading whatever material I've brought with me." As always, the hardest part is beginning. But once you start slogging through your assignment, the pain will slip away, you will hit your stride, and before you know it, your ride will have arrived and that once terrifying task will be safely completed.

Procrastination Battle Plan #4: *Build a routine*

Your schedule varies each day. But you should be able to identify at least one hour, on each weekday, that is consistently free. If you have an early class, make this the hour right after it lets out. If you have a late morning class, make this the hour right before it starts. In general, the morning and early afternoon are the best times to find these consistently free hours. Time in the late afternoon and evening is much more susceptible to being hijacked by unexpected events as your friends finish up their classes and start knocking on your door.

Once you've identified these protected hours, use them to do the same work each week. For example, maybe Mondays, Wednesdays, and Fridays are for chipping away at your History reading assignments, and Tuesdays and Thursdays are for making progress on your weekly Statistics problem set. The idea is to build a routine in which you use the same reserved time slot each week to do the same thing, with the goal of transforming these slices of work into a habit, something you no longer have to convince yourself to do.

"I figured out pretty early on the most annoying thing about bad habits—namely, their tenacity—could be very useful if it was applied to other things," explains Simon, a straight-A student from Brown. "I found that good habits, like making sure I do [certain work at the same time each week], are really hard to get rid of."

Unfortunately, these five hours a week are probably not enough to complete all of your work (if only that were true!). But they do represent five hours of productivity that didn't exist before. And, more important, the first work of the day breaks the seal on your motivation. Once you have accomplished one big task, it becomes much easier to tackle more. So follow Simon's advice, and let this simple good habit greatly reduce the effort required to launch a productive day.

Procrastination Battle Plan #5: *Choose your hard days*

Hard days are inescapable at college. Sometimes you simply have more work due than you can handle with a well-balanced schedule. In these cases, relaxation and socializing have to take a backseat to your study obligations. As Jeremy, a straight-A student from Dartmouth, admits: "Occasionally I end up setting aside one full day where I just lock myself in my room with some food and grind through it." You can't avoid these hard days, but you can control their impact.

If you see a large number of deadlines looming just over the horizon, you can be sure that there will be some hard days in your near future. Here's the secret: Plan them in advance. Don't wait until the deadlines are so close that you have no choice but to buckle down. Instead, scout out one or two days to preemptively designate as "hard." By choosing them ahead of time, you can space them out so that you never have two hard days in a row, and you won't be caught off guard by this sudden burst of intensity. Try to plan relaxing, nonacademic activities immediately before and after these days. This will ease their impact. As Jeremy explains: "If I work all day Saturday, I will let myself go out hard on Saturday night and take Sunday off."

In addition, you should prepare yourself mentally. Tell friends which days are going to be hard, warn them not to expect much communication from you, and ask for their encouragement. If all of your friends know that Tuesday is going to be a rough day for you, then you will be much more likely to keep busy and do the work. It would be embarrassing, after all, to talk up your upcoming hard day, garnering sympathy and support from friends, and then be discovered that afternoon, still in your boxers, experimenting with the use of your toes as an alternative to your missing remote control.

By proactively scheduling hard days on a regular basis, you reduce their negative impact. When you are forced into an all-day work marathon against your wishes, you feel drained and abused. If that same day has been planned and hyped for the past week, you'll come away feeling invigorated by your accomplishment. You expected the challenge, prepared for the challenge, and survived it. This strategy is more psychological than time saving, but the effect is powerful. Take ownership of your schedule and you are more likely to respect it.

Choose When, Where, and How Long

The little things count. This is especially true when it comes to studying. Before we get caught up in the details of exactly how to review and synthesize material, there are some basic questions that we must address first: *When* during the day should you study? *Where* should you go to study? *How long* should you study before taking a break? The right answers to these questions will boost your productivity, allowing you to squeeze more work out of even less time. The wrong answers will slow you down and make this process more difficult than it needs to be. Straight-A students, I found out, devote a lot of thought to these questions; they recognize how these seemingly little details can make or break their study efforts and have experimented extensively to discover the most effective strategies. Step #3 will walk you through the results of these experiments and present tested approaches for each of these three crucial study skills.

QUESTION: When is the best time to study?
ANSWER: *Early.*

"I like doing work in one big chunk upon getting back from class, or doing it in between classes, depending on my schedule," says Simon from Brown. "I try to never leave it until late at night." Simon's plan emphasizes an important reality about studying: You're most effective between when you wake up and when you eat dinner. You should accomplish as much work as possible during this time.

This advice runs counter to most students' instincts. To many, the evening seems ideal for work. Why? Because the morning and afternoon are crowded. Classes, meals, meetings, and other activities take over these hours, leaving few continuous periods for really settling in and getting things done. Night, on the other hand, seems like one long, uninterrupted stretch of good work time. Right? Wrong!

First, nighttime is not as long as you think. By the time you finish dinner, gather your materials, and finally begin your work, you really have only a few hours left before it becomes too late and your desire to sleep hijacks your concentration.

Second, nighttime is not as free as you think. It's prime time. Inevitably some can't-miss TV show nags for your attention, or the loud music of a party down the hall beckons seductively. Night is when people most want to socialize. You see movies at night. You go to parties at night. Shows, speakers, and other campus performances happen at night. People gather back at their dorm rooms to gossip and distract each other. Few among us have achieved the required level of nerd-dom necessary to resist such temptations—and we shouldn't have to.

Finally, nighttime is when your body begins to wind down. After a long day of activity, it's ready to begin a slow descent into sleep. Even before it gets late, the energy available to your mind has already declined. By 7:00 or 8:00 P.M., your focus is weak at best.

For these reasons, you must minimize the amount of work you do after dinner. At the same time, however, it's true that working during the day can also be complicated. As mentioned, there are few continuous stretches of free time in the morning and afternoon. Don't fear this fractured schedule. Bring your materials with you throughout the day, and fill in any small patches of free time with productive work. As Wendy, a straight-A student from Amherst, explains: "I try to take a book I need to read along with me all the time, in case some free time pops up while I'm doing something else." Doris, from Harvard, has a similar philosophy, admitting that she sneaks in work between meetings or classes, using small blocks of thirty or forty-five minutes at a time. If you follow this approach, you'll be surprised at the amount of work you can squeeze into your hectic daytime schedule.

The trick is to be efficient. If you have an hour in between classes, head straight from the first class to a library, or similar study location, near the second class. Mentally prepare yourself on the way over so that when you hit the study spot you can become productive within seconds. Also, be sure to avoid your dorm room or other public places as much as possible during the day. You need to separate your work mind-set from your relaxation mind-set. By hanging around your room, or the student center, you are much more likely to become distracted and let a potentially productive work period slip away at the expense of a mundane conversation. Become a ghost during the day. Like an academic ninja, slip from hidden study spot to hidden study spot, leaving only an eerie trail of completed work behind you (see the next question, *"Where should you study?"* for more advice on choosing the right locations).

The idea here is not to become antisocial. When you're done for the day, feel free to go have fun! Party like a demon. You aren't missing out on an important social event by avoiding some half-assed gossip between classes. The more meaningful experiences will happen later, at the frats or in your dorm room after everyone is done with classes for the day. Remember: *"Work hard, play hard"* is always better than *"Work kind of hard, play kind of hard."*

In addition to the extra energy and better focus that you gain by studying early, the spread-out nature of this schedule makes it less of a strain. Working for forty-five minutes, running to class, working for an hour, going to another class, then working another forty-five minutes before grabbing lunch is much less odious then sitting down and working for two and a half hours straight. This approach also makes optimal use of your time. Most students simply waste these free chunks during the day. By taking advantage of daytime study pockets, you're freeing up valuable nighttime hours to go out and have the sort of fun that defines the college experience.

QUESTION: **Where should you study?**
ANSWER: *In isolation.*

Identify a number of isolated study spots spread out across campus and rotate through these hidden locations when you study. Any place in your dorm or house is off-limits, as are the big public study spaces in your main library. As Greta from Dartmouth explains: "If you stay in your dorm, it seems like no one is studying...because they aren't." This atmosphere is not conducive to concentration. Look for less-visited libraries away from the center of campus, and search out carrels high up in the stacks or buried down in the basement. Always keep your eyes open for the next great hidden study spot—small libraries in the buildings of student organizations, a hole-in-the-wall coffee shop, or the local public library are all potential concentration gold mines.

You need multiple locations for two reasons. First, as you move through your day, squeezing in study sessions between classes, it's nice to always know of a nearby study spot. Second, changing locations prevents you from burning out at any one place. This is the strategy followed by Doris from Harvard, who explains: "to keep my mind stimulated, I regularly rotate between different venues."

The isolation of these spots is important for the obvious reason: It shields you from distraction. That little procrastination devil on your shoulder is an incredible salesman. If you give him even a glimpse of an alternative to your work, then he will close the deal. To neutralize this devil, isolate him. Don't let him see your couch, the cute girls tossing Frisbees on the quad, or your friends chatting in your dorm room lounge. If you cut yourself off from the outside world during your work hours, then you have a much better chance of completing what needs to get done, and, as an added bonus, the resulting increase in concentration will help you get your work done faster.

Many students will admit that there is something a bit dramatic about working in exaggerated isolation. It may sound corny, but

quarantining yourself in a study bunker seems to increase the importance of the work you are about to tackle. You can almost imagine
the voice of a grave military officer saying, "Son, we're all counting on
you . . . good luck," as you head off to your silent nook. This kind of
gravitas is lacking when you flop down on your couch with a textbook propped up on your chest and your roommate in the chair next
to you struggling to learn an obnoxious Dave Matthews song on his
out-of-tune guitar. As Christine from Harvard states plainly: "Studying in bed has never worked."

These mind games are not trite. Don't underestimate the importance of psychology in becoming an effective student. Almost every
straight-A student interviewed for this book followed some variant
of this isolation strategy. Some went so far as to wear earplugs or
travel great distances from campus to eliminate any chance of distraction. They understood the mental edge their surroundings provided—and you should, too.

QUESTION: How long should you study?
ANSWER: *No more than one hour at a time without
a break.*

Your break needs to be only five to ten minutes, but it's important
that you take an intellectual breather during this period. This means
you should find something you can concentrate on, for just a few
minutes, which has nothing to do with the work you were completing right before the break. Read a newspaper article or send a few
e-mails. That should be enough. This disengagement helps refresh
your mind and facilitates the process of finding new angles and in-

sights when you begin your work again. Some students brought a novel or newspaper with them, and then read a chapter or an article at every break. Others chose a project for the day—perhaps writing a long e-mail to a friend they hadn't seen in ages, or building a list of options for an upcoming vacation—that they could work on bit by bit with each break they took.

Even when you feel like you are on a roll, keep taking regular breaks. Over the long run, it will maximize your energy and retention of the material. As Laura from Dartmouth recounts: "I swear I get more done taking regular breaks than I would if I just worked straight through."

Why does this timing work the best? I don't know exactly. Some cognitive science research concludes that about fifty minutes is the optimal learning period to maximize the material synthesized per time unit. For example, the Web site for the IPFW Center for Academic Support and Advancement states: "Studies suggest you should study in 40 or 50 minute increments for maximum retention. After approximately 40 minutes, take a short break (5 minutes) and continue studying. Without a break, retention is about 30% after 2 hours."* But we don't have to get bogged down with these scientific details. The main reason I advocate this timing is because almost every straight-A student interviewed for this book followed a similar plan. When asked how long they studied in a single sitting, all but a few of their answers fell somewhere between half an hour and an hour:

"Not more than an hour," replied Chris.

---

*http://www.ipfw.edu/casa/SI/sistudy.html

"One hour, then I get up and do something else for a bit," replied Melanie.

"About forty minutes to an hour," replied Ryan.

"One hour on, fifteen minutes off," replied Lydia.

"One to one and a half hours. Then I would always take a break," replied Lacey.

And the list goes on, as response after response revealed a similar strategy. The point here should be clear: Through trial and error, dozens of high-performing students have individually stumbled across this same technique—study for an hour, then take a break—so you should trust it too.

Part One Cheat Sheet

Step #1. Manage Your Time in Five Minutes a Day

- Jot down to-dos and deadlines on a list whenever they arise.
- Transfer these to-dos and deadlines to your calendar every morning.
- Plan your day each morning by labeling your to-dos with realistic time frames and moving what you don't have time for to different dates.

Step #2. Declare War on Procrastination

- Keep a work progress journal, and every day record what you wanted to accomplish and whether or not you succeeded.
- When working, eat healthy snacks to maximize your energy.
- Transform horrible tasks into a big event to help you gather the energy to start.
- Build work routines to make steady progress on your obligations without expending too much of your limited motivational resources.
- Choose your hard days in advance to minimize their impact.

Step #3. Choose When, Where, and How Long

- Try to fit as much work as possible into the morning and afternoon, between classes and obligations.
- Study in isolated locations.
- Take a break every hour.

Part 2

Quizzes
and Exams

"Students who develop
superior study skIlls
can do more in less time."

Rielle, *a straight-A college student*

Here's a simple truth: *Most college students are terrible at studying.*

It's not really their fault. When students arrive at college, they're on their own. No one ever takes them aside to teach them the right way to study, so most students just make it up as they go along. For example, when an exam date looms, the typical student pulls out his books and notes and then cloisters himself in his dorm study lounge or at the desk in his room. At this point, he begins reviewing, almost at random, poring over as many notes and chapters as he can manage, with frequent breaks to converse with friends and check e-mail, until, finally, his will to continue completely flickers out. If he's particularly industrious, he might manage to pull an all-nighter. Otherwise, he'll probably call it quits by midnight. The next day, he takes the exam, bleary-eyed, completely unsure of what grade to expect. Occasionally, this approach earns him an A-, but, for the most part, he remains wearily ensconced in the world of Bs and the occasional C.

There are two problems with this approach. First, there's the *timing*. In Part One, I introduced the term "pseudo-work" to describe this unfortunate habit of studying in long, low-intensity, fatigue-saturated marathons of pain. To counter this behavior, we discussed some intelligent time-management strategies to help you spread out your work into small, high-intensity bursts.

The second problem with this approach is the *technique*. As shown in the scenario above, the typical student studies by performing rote review—the reading and rereading of assignments and notes as many times as possible. The idea behind this strategy is that somehow, if the material crosses before your eyes enough times, the key ideas will stick around long enough to be later regurgitated during the exam. Here's the problem with rote review: It's a horrible way to study.

First of all, it doesn't work. Even though you spend a lot of time, you don't end up actually learning the material well. Methodically trying to reread every source covered in class is an incredibly inefficient way to prepare. And because it's boring, your mind quickly fatigues, and once your mind shuts down, you can forget about synthesizing complicated arguments. To successfully learn even a modest amount of information using this technique requires an absurd number of hours. The second problem with rote review is that it's really painful. There is no way around it: Cramming is mind numbing, especially when you have a hopelessly large amount of material to review.

Here's the good news: It doesn't have to be this way. Not convinced? What follows are real quotes from some of the straight-A students interviewed for this book:

- "I never do all-nighters."

- "I have a great deal of free time."

- "Balance is very important for me."

- "I have tons of free time nearly every day."

- "[I worked hard at first,] but by junior and senior year I was having a blast."

- "I spent relatively little time in college doing homework or reading."

- "I get my work done quickly in the morning and then have plenty of time for uninterrupted playing."

Many students find these claims hard to believe because they contradict a cherished piece of conventional wisdom: *High-scoring students must be grinds.* Where does this belief come from? For one thing, as Matthew, a straight-A student from Brown, explains: "There *are* people who devote their lives to The Grind." And these students tend to be very visible. They complain incessantly about the amount of work they have to do, constantly check in with their friends to compare study hours, and can be seen camped out in the library during most times of the day. If you encounter enough of these public grinds, it can begin to seem like they represent what is necessary to achieve academic success.

However, there is another, more insidious reason why this belief persists. **Most students incorrectly believe rote review is the only way to study.** Think about this for a moment: If you assume that all studying is equal, then the conclusion that all straight-A students are grinds becomes unavoidable. We noted earlier that making high grades with rote review requires an absurd number of hours; therefore, if rote review is the only way to study, then high-scoring students *must* be studying a lot more than the average student.

This is why, before we continue, you must first understand and accept this crucial fact: **There are many, many different ways to study (and rote review is not one of the better ones).** Once you reject the idea that all studying is equal, and instead make the crucial connection that studying is like any other skill—and as with any skill, it can be done well or done poorly—then the premise of this book starts to make sense. Non-grind straight-A students are not unexplainable or incredible. They have simply mastered, either through aggressive trial and error or interactions with older straight-A students, study strategies that are far superior to rote review.

Let me put it another way. If we make an analogy between college and professional basketball, then the rote-reviewing students are all shooting the ball underhand granny style, while the non-grind straight-A students are those who've figured out how to shoot a jump shot. It doesn't matter if the rote reviewers practice those granny shots twice as many hours as the straight-A students; when it's game time, the jump shooters are going to score a lot more points. Better technique trumps more effort.

Part Two will teach you, in essence, how to shoot an academic jump shot. It covers the nuts and bolts of smart exam preparation—the many small techniques, refined by straight-A students over countless semesters, that add up to a much better way to study. Forget everything you think you know about preparing for exams, and approach the steps that follow with an open mind. Some of this advice will make immediate sense, some will seem obvious, and some will surprise you. But just remember that these tactics are not arbitrary, they are not based on one guy's experience, and they certainly are not abstract theories spouted by some self-proclaimed expert. Instead, they are the realistic strategies developed by real straight-A students to ace tests under the harsh demands of a college workload. If you combine these tested study skills with the time-management techniques taught in Part One, you will find yourself scoring higher, learning more, and studying less than you previously thought possible.

Quizzes vs. Exams

In general, all of the advice described in Part Two will work for both quizzes and exams. But in the case of quizzes, it's not always necessary to put in quite as much effort (though it certainly doesn't hurt).

But first things first—let's get our definitions correct. Keep in mind that professors often use the terms *quiz* and *exam* interchangeably, so forget what they say and make your own determination about a given test. Here's a simple rule to follow: **If the test is worth less than 15 percent of your final grade, it's a quiz; otherwise, it's an exam. If the test is worth only 5 percent or less of your grade, designate this a *tiny quiz*.**

Don't spend too much time on tiny quizzes. Even if you fail one, it still probably won't change your final letter grade. And if you're attending classes and keeping up with your reading, you should be able to score above average with little to no preparation.

For larger quizzes, you can more or less follow the advice in this section as written, but feel free to move more quickly through the review-focused steps (Steps #3 and #4). If you don't master every last topic that might be covered on a quiz, that's okay. A missed question here or there won't make a big difference on your final grade. And if you treat every quiz like a midterm, you're going to overload your schedule. Quizzes are checkups, not comprehensive evaluations, so treat them as such.

The only exception, of course, is if your grade is in danger. If you're in academic trouble, perhaps due to a poor performance on a previous exam or paper, then go all out in your review. If you apply the full force of the study strategies that follow, you will be guaranteed to knock any quiz out of the park.

Step 1

Take Smart Notes

First things first: Always go to class! The importance of this rule cannot be overemphasized. It doesn't matter if your class meets at 6:00 A.M., at the top of the steepest hill on campus, on Saturday mornings—wake up, get dressed, and get to the lecture on time. As Lydia, a straight-A student from Dartmouth, explains, if you skip class, "it'll take twice as long studying to make up for what you missed." This is why class attendance is so important. Not because learning is power, or it's what your parents would want you to do, but because it saves you time. If you attend class regularly, you will significantly cut down on the amount of studying required to score high grades. Don't make this negotiable. Even if you're tired, hung over, or extremely busy, find a way to make it there.

Of course, just going to class isn't enough by itself. To reduce your study time, you have to also take good notes once you're there. Keep this in mind: Note-taking is an art form. Doing it well requires expert guidance, and fortunately there is no better place to look for expert guidance than real straight-A students. Here are their proven note-taking strategies.

Gather the Right Materials

When I was a freshman, less than half of my class brought a laptop to campus. The year I graduated, over 95 percent of incoming freshmen brought laptops. By the time you read this, laptops will more or less be the de facto standard for undergraduates across the country, and this is a great advancement for the cause of collegiate note-taking. Why? I think David, another Dartmouth student, put it best: "Use your laptop. *Seriously!* You will be overwhelmed by the quality and legibility of your notes . . . it's really a no-brainer."

Yes, it may seem somewhat geeky. But it's becoming increasingly common, and besides, the academic advantages far outweigh any minor social stigma. As mentioned by David: You type much faster than you write, so the laptop will allow you to record more points in more detail. This increased detail and readability will make it easier to study come test time—and that should be all you need to hear.

If you don't have a laptop, then make sure you have one notebook for every class and a pen that you are comfortable with. Try to write clearly. You might even consider typing summaries of your notes at the end of each week. I sometimes followed this strategy in my pre-laptop days, and found that it saved me significant study time in the long run.

There is, however, one obvious exception to this laptop rule: For math, science, economics, and engineering courses that are heavy on numbers and equations, pencil and paper are acceptable. Some people are comfortable approximating complicated mathematical symbols on their laptop, while others are not. If you fall into the latter category, don't worry about using a notebook; for a technical course, the difference between the two mediums is less important.

Finally, you should also have one folder for each class. Every piece of paper you receive during a lecture—outlines, assignment descriptions, reading excerpts—should be dated and put in this folder. The same goes for graded problem sets and papers. The folders will make it much easier to find materials when you need them later for review.

A lot of "experts" recommend needlessly complicated additions to this basic material list. They talk of using multiple colored pens, special notebooks, and organized class binders equipped with portable three-hole punches. Real straight-A students ignore this nonsense. As Anna, a straight-A Dartmouth student, warns: "A lot of students focus on making their notebooks look pretty and then forget about the content." Put your notes on your laptop and your loose papers in a folder, and you'll be fine.

Take Smart Notes in Nontechnical Courses (What's the Big Idea?)

A "nontechnical course" refers to any course outside of math, science, economics, and engineering. We're talking about English, history, psychology, political science, anthropology, classics, education— basically anything that doesn't make frequent use of mathematical formulas. These courses are the domain of ridiculously long reading assignments and dignified professors lecturing from behind a podium.

The key to doing well in these courses is straightforward: **Identify the big ideas.** That's what it all comes down to. Exams in nontechnical courses focus entirely on big ideas—they require you to explain them, contrast them, and reevaluate them in the light of new evidence. If you are aware of, and understand, all of the big ideas presented in the course, these tasks are not so difficult, and strong grades will follow.

As you would expect, lectures are a major source of these big ideas. Identifying them, however, is not a trivial task. Professors ramble. And they rarely start a class by clearly identifying the big ideas that will be explored. Instead, they tend to dive right in, leaving the poor student to separate on his own the interesting conclusions from the digressions.

"A whole lot of superfluous things are said in each class," explains Jeremy, a straight-A student from Dartmouth. "You have to learn how to pick out which is which." This is hard, and as such, most students don't take very good notes in nontechnical courses, which has major ramifications when it comes time to study. If your notes don't already clearly identify the big ideas, then you are going to be forced to try to figure them out from scratch while reviewing. Allow me to spoil this particular ending for you: Unless you set aside dozens of hours to prepare, you're not going to accomplish this task, and your grade on the exam becomes a crapshoot. If the exam happens to ask questions that deal with the random assortment of ideas that you do know, then you might do okay, but if it happens to ask questions that deal with many of the big ideas that you never learned, then you will do poorly.

Obviously, you want to avoid this situation. The solution is to figure out how to take notes that clearly identify and explain all of the big ideas that are presented so that you can review them later without spending any extra time. Let's jump right into the details of how to accomplish this goal.

Format Your Notes Aggressively

When you first arrive at the classroom, date your notes and record the title of the day's lecture, if it's available. If you're using a laptop, create a separate *notes* directory for each class. Save your document in this folder with the date in the file name. This will make it easier to organize the material when you review.

When it comes to formatting the text itself, the basic rule to follow is that anything that makes the information easier to read is fair game. You don't need a consistent scheme. Don't be afraid to use aggressive text formatting to help emphasize important points. On a computer, smart students often make use of bold fonts and lists to help organize their thoughts. When using a pen and paper, underlining, indentations, drawing boxes around ideas, and bullet points also help structure the information. If you're defining a word, make it bold. If you're writing down an exception to the last observation you recorded, start with: **"HOWEVER: . . ."** Christine, a straight-A Harvard student, suggests that you "develop your own shorthand— 'esp.' for 'especially,' 'N.A.' for 'North America,' etc." Skip lines with wild abandon, use tabs freely, change the font size, write entire sentences in all caps, throw around asterisks like penny candy—

have fun and do whatever helps you visualize the important concepts.

"Your notes are for you and you alone," explains Lee, a straight-A Columbia student. "They don't have to make sense to anyone else."

Capture Big Ideas by Using the Question/ Evidence/Conclusion Structure

The central challenge to note-taking in nontechnical courses is deciding *what* to write down. Some students attempt to record the lecture verbatim. *Don't do this.* "The best advice I can give on note-taking," explains Doris, a straight-A student from Harvard, "is not to try to write down everything the professor says, because that is both impossible and counterproductive." Put simply: You can't write that fast! And you will end up expending too much energy capturing exact words as opposed to identifying big ideas. Instead, remember the following structure:

Question

Evidence

Conclusion

Most big ideas in nontechnical courses are presented in this structure. Why? Professional academics think in terms of questions. This is how they see the world. To them, in order to find big ideas, you must first find questions and then follow a path of evidence to a corresponding conclusion.

Accordingly, this is also how professors lecture. They offer up questions and then walk you through various pieces of evidence en route to an interesting conclusion. **You should take advantage of this**

reality by recording all your notes in a Question/Evidence/Conclusion format.

The basics of this approach are simple. All of the information you write down during class should be associated with a well-labeled question. Each question should be paired with a well-labeled conclusion. When you're done, your notes for a given lecture should consist only of a bunch of question/conclusion pairs, each separated by points of evidence that support why the conclusion is a reasonable answer to the question. In other words, your goal is to fit all the facts and observations spewed out during class into this nice simple structure.

Keep in mind that professors don't always state the question. Often they jump right into the evidence and leave it to you to deduce the question being discussed. Don't be afraid to jot down **"QUESTION:"** and then leave the rest of the line blank as you begin recording evidence. Once you figure out what the professor's talking about, you can go back and fill in this blank.

The same holds true for conclusions. Professors will sometimes hint at a conclusion but not come right out and present a neat endpoint for the current discussion. In this case, it will be up to you to synthesize the question, evidence, and professor's hints into a conclusion of your own. This is the important part. When you formulate a conclusion, you are cementing a big idea. If you can't finalize a conclusion before the professor moves on to the next question, simply jot down **"CONCLUSION:"** and plan to come back later during a lull in the lecture, or immediately following class, to fill in the blank.

Something to remember: Conclusions are rarely simple. Professors often offer conclusions that only summarize the complexity of the issue. Consider, for example, the following question from a literature class: "Who was the greatest novelist of the twentieth century?" A simple conclusion might be: "Hemingway." And the evidence, in this case, might be several points highlighting the influence and originality of Hemingway's work. On the other hand, it's much more likely that a college professor would offer up a more complicated conclusion to this question, perhaps something like: "Different generations answered this question differently, depending on the prevailing social issues of their time." In this case, the evidence could be excerpts from scholars of various periods talking about their favorite novelists, as well as some observations concerning the differing social climates during each of these eras.

The more classes you take, the better you will become at summarizing a complicated conclusion. In the beginning, don't be afraid to ask questions to help figure out if your conclusions are correct or not. If you're shy, go up to the professor after class or become a regular during his office hours. Professors love this kind of student interaction. Use it to help polish your conclusion-sleuthing skills.

Another important tip: Take full advantage of lulls in the lecture. As hinted above, some professors shoot out information so fast that there doesn't seem to be enough time to jot down every question or think about every conclusion. Sometimes it takes all of your energy just to keep up with the evidence. In this case, wait for slow spots. When the professor wanders off on a personal anecdote, or a student interrupts with an inane question, use this time to hurriedly go back and clean up what you have been throwing down. Record conclusions, clarify questions, and add illustrative formatting to pieces of evidence. If you're not rushed, spend five minutes after class to polish your notes before packing up. As Doris from Harvard explains: "It's important to read over your notes right after class to absorb them and make corrections and additions, otherwise you'll be susceptible to entirely forgetting what was covered that day." These little moments and adjustments will make a big difference when it comes time to review.

Finally, remember that the number of questions presented in a discussion can vary significantly, depending on the class. One professor may spend an entire lecture exploring a single question, whereas another may move through a dozen small questions in the space of an hour. Often, a professor will introduce a major question for the whole lecture and then spend the time exploring smaller questions that help build toward an overarching conclusion. Again, the more classes you take, the more intuitive these structures will become. "If you pay attention to the contours of a professor's lecture," explains Matthew from Brown, "you can determine what he feels is important." Listen for pauses, which usually follow key points, and remember that personal anecdotes are often spun during less important parts of the class.

In general, there is no right or wrong way to break up a particular lecture into question/conclusion pairs, so just find a structure that more or less works. Feel free to mess around with your notes as you go along. Add or remove questions on the fly. If certain evidence doesn't seem to fit with any particular question, no matter how hard you try, that's okay, just label it as such. Professors have been known to wander. By simply *attempting* to associate all information with questions and conclusions, you are already a large step ahead of most students when it comes to understanding and internalizing the big ideas.

A Brief Example

Presented below is an excerpt from a real college lecture on the decline and fall of the Roman Empire. It's followed by an example of how a straight-A student might take notes on this discussion. Keep in mind that the student here would have probably first recorded the evidence bullet points on the fly and then gone back later to fill in the question and conclusion once he had a better idea of where the professor was heading. Also note that the evidence features a lot of aggressive formatting: It's split up into lists, with words often bolded and capitalized to emphasize their importance. There is no consistent scheme being applied here. The formatting is just what might come naturally to the student during the heat of the moment, to help him understand and underscore the concepts being presented.

Lecture Excerpt:

The focus of today's lecture is what is called the "decline and fall" of the Roman Empire. The idea that the Roman Empire "fell" to the savage, barbarian hordes has been a popular one ever since the eighteenth century. Edward Gibbon's book by that title pointed to two causes, in his mind, of Rome's decline and fall: Christians and barbarians. Sometimes he even confused the two. Gibbon argued that Christianity attracted the least intellectual and most superstitious elements in the empire, and that not surprisingly did the triumph of

Christianity in the Empire coincide with the downfall of Rome. Christians, according to Gibbon, undermined with their ideas of forgiveness and mercy, the severe patriotic virtues of the Romans that had enabled them to resist heroically the barbarian invasions. Rostovsteff and Toynbee had a similar argument, but instead of blaming the Christians, they looked for social and political causes. Both argued that sometime in the third century, the Roman ruling elite lost its political and intellectual nerve and allowed lesser elements to take over who were much less capable of holding the empire together under the onslaught of barbarians.

All of these historians, however, looked at the history of Rome in the years 250–500 from a point of view that geographically was very narrow. These historians lived, after all, in a world where the center of European civilization was no longer the Mediterranean Sea, but Northwestern Europe. They focused, then, on what France and Britain looked like in the 6th century A.D., and assumed that Northwest Europe was the natural heir to classical antiquity. In fact, only in the Latin West was there anything like a decline and fall, and even there the collapse was administrative. It was not an immediate or huge catastrophe, but a gradual ebb of Roman influence over those areas that had begun in the 3rd century.

"The 'Decline and Fall' of the Roman Empire," copyright 2000 by Philip Gavitt, Professor of History, St. Louis University, St. Louis, Missouri.

(Online at: http://www.slu.edu/colleges/AS/cmrs/0221002.html)

Notes on excerpt:

QUESTION: Was there really a big "fall" of the Roman Empire?

- Roman Empire having a catastrophic decline and fall, at the hands of savage barbarians, popular idea since eighteenth century.

- **Edward Gibbon**—wrote book blaming fall on Christians and barbarians. Christian beliefs replaced heroic virtues, weakened military, let barbarians take over.

- **Rostovsteff and Toynbee**—wrote books with similar arguments
  - EXCEPT: Not Christians' fault, but social and political problems that led to weak empire.

- **HOWEVER:** These views are "geographically narrow."
  - Authors lived in Europe, so they focused on Europe, only place where it looked like Empire had a big fall.
  - Loss of power in Mediterranean region not nearly so pronounced . . . no real big decline and fall there.

CONCLUSION: The idea of a catastrophic decline and fall of the Roman Empire became popular in European circles, but it overstates reality . . . too much emphasis on what happened to the Empire in Europe.

The Discussion Exception

Nontechnical courses will occasionally make use of the class discussion format, in which the professor lets the students lead a discussion on a preselected topic or group of topics. The note-taking strategies described above will not fit this environment. When students lead a discussion, you should no longer expect neatly packaged big ideas. Instead, you end up with a lot of random observations surrounding the occasional gem, so in this circumstance, employ the following simplified note-taking strategy:

Clearly label the topic of the discussion. If a student makes a point that strikes you as insightful, jot it down. If *you* think up a point that strikes you as insightful, first jot it down, then raise your hand and offer it to the class. Participation keeps you focused. If a student says something you feel is mistaken or irrelevant, just ignore it. And, most important, if the professor chimes in, write down what he says and underline it several times. You better believe that his points are insightful. By the end of class, you will be left with a topic followed by a relatively short list of interesting insights. That's all you need. Discussions are supposed to help jog your thinking and perhaps offer interesting ideas for upcoming paper assignments. This approach to note-taking focuses on that goal by identifying only interesting insights and encouraging you to synthesize your own.

Take Smart Notes in Technical Courses (Where's the Problem?)

Technical courses describe any subject that makes heavy use of mathematical formulas or computer code—for example, math, science, engineering, economics, computer science, and quantitative social science. The note-taking strategies for these courses differ significantly from the strategies we just covered for nontechnical courses. In fact, the strategies here are actually much simpler. As Greta, a straight-A student from Dartmouth, explains, for technical courses you should focus on "capturing lots of detailed explanations of problems . . . the more notes the better." In other words, you can forget about big ideas. **The key to taking notes in a technical course is to record as many sample problems as possible.** When you study, these sample problems will prove to be your most important resource. Accordingly, your entire focus in a technical class should be to write down, as faithfully as possible, the steady stream of examples provided by your professor. Let's take a closer look at how to do this:

Don't Read Your Assignments, but Do Keep Them Handy

Most technical courses have assigned reading. These readings are usually textbook chapters, and they typically focus on a specific technique or formula. **Don't do this reading.** It may sound blasphemous, but it's the reality of college-level technical courses: Very few students actually do the technical reading ahead of time. Why? Because the exact same material will be covered in class. If you don't understand a topic *after* it's presented by the professor, then you can go back and use the reading to help fill in the blanks. This ordering of events is much more efficient.

What you should do, however, is bring your reading to class. Smart students follow the professor's examples with their textbook open. This significantly improves your understanding of the techniques the first time they are presented, and it helps sharpen your questions when you get lost. Make sure that you have your assigned reading material gathered and ready to go before class begins.

Prioritize Your Note-taking

In a perfect world, you would successfully capture every single problem discussed in class, as well as every single answer, and all the steps in between. Don't expect this to happen. Professors move too quickly for you to record all of their examples, so you must learn to prioritize your note-taking.

First priority: *Record the problem statement and answer.*

Even in the fastest class, there should be time to jot down the questions and final solutions. If you're in the middle of writing down steps when the professor gives the answer and moves on to the next problem, skip the rest of the steps, record the answer, and move on too. You can try to come back during a lull to fill in more of the steps (so leave space), but even if you don't, having only the problem and answer will still be useful for review later.

Second priority: *Question the confusing.*

Students who do well in technical courses are those who closely follow the problems being presented and then insist on asking questions when they don't understand a specific step. Is this annoying? A little bit. Does it really improve your understanding of the techniques being presented? Absolutely. If you can't ask a question, then at least clearly mark where you got confused. Write a bunch of question marks or circle the line in your notes; this will help you later when you study. Remember, however, the more questions you get answered in class, the less legwork you will have to do later. So raise your hand, be confident, and ask away!

Third priority: *Record the steps of the sample problem.*

The reality of technical courses is that the professor usually goes slow only on the first sample problem presented for a new technique. These are usually the only sample problems for which you can capture all of the steps. So pay particular attention at the beginning of the discussion, and don't get discouraged if subsequent problems fly by too fast for you to record all of the intermediate steps.

Final priority: *Annotate the steps.*

If you get ahead of the professor on a given problem, and you have time to kill, annotate the steps with little explanations of what they accomplish or why they're important. In the cases where you do have time for these annotations, they will prove immensely useful when you review.

Step 2

Demote Your Assignments

Most students spend way too much time on reading assignments and problem sets, causing them to feel constantly overwhelmed by their work. This is a problem. If day-to-day assignments dominate your schedule, then there is no time left to prepare properly for the bigger exams and projects.

Straight-A students hate excessive schoolwork just as much as the next student, which is why they have mastered the art of minimizing the time spent on assignments while still learning exactly what they need to know. This chapter details their strategies for powering through readings and problem sets with a minimum of stress. Follow this advice, and your assignments will be reduced from a source of energy-draining tedium into manageable tasks you can actually learn from.

Work Constantly

Most college students depend on "day-before" assignment planning, meaning they never start an assignment until the day before it's due. This might be the simplest scheduling decision, but it creates many problems. Large assignments will quickly transform from potentially interesting to tedious to painful when tackled in one monolithic, last-minute chunk of time. And, if two or more assignments happen to be due on the same day (which will happen often), you will be forced into a frenzied work marathon that will produce lackluster results at best.

Smart students avoid these issues by working constantly on assignments, in small chunks, every day. "I try to sit down every Sunday night and plan out the week," explains Simon, a straight-A student from Brown. "My goal is to make sure that I don't have too much work on busy days and that I do at least a little bit each day."

For example, if you have a problem set due every week, complete one problem a day, one hour at a time. Don't spend five hours the night before. The same goes for reading assignments—knock off a chapter a day, and you'll never find yourself spending a lonely night with a textbook and a six-pack of Red Bull.

Bear in mind that even if you get caught up on all of your assignments for a given class, you should continue to work. For example, if it's Sunday morning and you have already finished your reading for Monday's history class, and you have time to spare, break out a book and do a little of the reading for Wednesday's history class. This doesn't mean that you should study like crazy twenty-four hours a day. Don't stay up until 2 A.M. Sunday night trying to finish the entire week's load. But on days where you happen to be ahead of schedule, and you have already put aside time to work on a certain class, take advantage of this fortuitous situation to get ahead. Once you get used to working a little bit every day, you'll be surprised by how often this situation might arise.

Straight-A students use this strategy whenever the opportunity presents itself, since getting ahead on class work frees up time to focus on big projects like paper writing or test preparation. It may seem superstitious, but easy weeks never seem to come in pairs. They're like the calm before a storm: If you find yourself with time to spare, start getting ahead on your obligations, as a hurricane of deadlines is probably lurking just over the horizon.

Don't Read Everything

"Doing all of your reading in college is a luxury most of us can't afford—especially if you're involved in extracurriculars," explains Tyler, a straight-A student from Duke. "It's important to triage your assignments: What do you need to read? What do you need to skim? And what can you skip entirely?" Lee from Columbia puts it as follows: "Reading can get overwhelming, and very few people I know do it all—that could drive a man insane!" And Chris, a straight-A student from Dartmouth, states his advice simply: "Don't read everything on the syllabus, of course."

These students all emphasize the same important point: It's impossible to read every single thing assigned to you in every class. Sometimes you are simply given more pages to cover than you have hours in the day to complete. Therefore, it will help you to remember the following: **Don't do all of your reading.** Colleges should mount this slogan on big bronze plaques and hang them up in every dorm room on campus—if every college freshman knew this secret, it would probably prevent a lot of unnecessary panic attacks.

The hard part, of course, is deciding what reading is important and what can be skipped. A lot of this decision-making ability comes from practice—the more college classes you take, the better you will become at identifying the exact level of importance of every assignment. There are, however, some general tips that can help you pick up this talent sooner rather than later. The techniques that follow are used by straight-A students to systematically identify which readings to spend time on and which to ignore.

For example, in most college courses there are one or two sources that show up on the reading list for almost every lecture. We will call these *favored sources*—they're usually a textbook or a course reader, and they provide the basic structure for the course by outlining key facts and arguments in a condensed form. **Always read the assignments from favored sources**.

Professors usually augment these favored sources with a variety of supplemental readings that provide context or analyze certain arguments and events in more detail. These supplemental readings are often academic papers, transcripts of speeches, or chapters from books—and they are typically fascinating. But they are also typically expendable, and you should not plan on reading them all. Instead, if your time is limited during a particular week, then your strategy should be to select only the most important supplemental readings for review.

Of course, college is about learning, and if you have time to get through all of the assigned reading, then you definitely should. Your professor selected all of these readings because he or she felt they were important for your complete understanding of the given topic, and the more you read, the smarter you become. But as Tyler stated earlier, reading everything assigned is a "luxury" that you can't always afford.

So how do you decide which supplemental readings to review, which to skim, and which to skip? Straight-A students follow this simple hierarchy:

Readings that **make an argument** are more important than

readings that **describe an event or person**, which are more important than

readings that only **provide context** (i.e., speech transcripts, press clippings).

Assignments at the top of this hierarchy require at least enough attention to allow you to identify the argument being made. They don't have to be read as carefully as a favored source, but you should spend enough time with them to gain a good understanding of their theses. Assignments in the middle of the hierarchy merit skimming, since they introduce facts that can clarify relevant arguments. A quick pass through should highlight enough of these facts to be useful, and you certainly don't need to carefully review every detail. Assignments at the bottom can usually be skipped, since professors will discuss what's important about them during class. Make sure, therefore, that you bring these readings to class and take careful notes.

Now let's look at a couple of sample entries from real college syllabi to illustrate how to apply this strategy in practice.

Example #1

The following entry comes from the syllabus of a history course titled The Emergence of Modern America.

Class #20: Vietnam

Reading:

Maier, Pauline, et al. (2003) *Inventing America*. New York: Norton, 952–957, 968–971.

Johnson, Lyndon B. (1992) "Speech at Johns Hopkins University," in George Katsiaficas, ed., *Vietnam Documents: American and Vietnamese Views of the War*. Armonk, N.Y.: Sharpe, 200–205. [electronic reserve]

O'Brien, Tim. (1998) "On the Rainy River," in *The Things They Carried*. New York: Random House, 39–61.

Let's assume that your schedule is swamped when you come across this assignment listing. What should you do? First, note that readings from *Inventing America* (a textbook) show up for almost every lecture in this syllabus, so this is clearly a favored source. Following our rule from above, you should definitely read the pages assigned from this textbook. The two other assignments look like supplemental readings, so let's apply our importance hierarchy to figure out how much attention to devote to each.

The Lyndon Johnson speech looks like a source of context, the lowest rung on our importance hierarchy. Your best bet in this case is to print out a copy and bring it with you to class. This way, if the professor makes some important points regarding Johnson's rhetoric, you can follow along and make notes on the pages. But don't bother giving it more than a quick skim in advance.

The Tim O'Brien excerpt comes from a great book. It's a semificationalized account of the draft during the Vietnam era, and it was a finalist for the Pulitzer Prize. Again, if you had the time, it would definitely be worth doing a careful reading of this excerpt, since it's likely to be the most engaging and colorful. But if you happen to be overloaded at this point, you need to apply the importance hierarchy. Because this is a description of an event, it's only on the second rung. Therefore, these twenty-two pages require a quick ten- to twenty-minute skim at best. As always, however, bring the book to class. If the professor mentions specific points relating to the book, you want to be able to follow along.

It should be noted that fiction is tricky. In this case, the Tim O'Brien book was a fictional account of a historical moment, and it's assigned in a history course concerned mainly with the cultural construction of modern America. In this context, the book is providing background to the discussion, not presenting arguments, and thus it falls clearly onto the second rung of our importance hierarchy. This is not, however, always true with fiction. Novels can also be used as vehicles for powerful cultural statements or explorations into why certain events transpired. In these cases, the fiction becomes a favored source, or, at the very least, it moves to the top of our supplemental hierarchy. For example, in a political science course dealing with totalitarianism in the twentieth century, George Orwell's *1984* is not a source of background, nor does it simply contextualize a historical moment; it instead presents an important argument on the subject. Keep this in mind when selecting your reading. Fiction should not, by any means, be automatically discounted. And if you are in an English class that focuses only on fiction, then obviously fiction readings are your favored sources. As Christine from Harvard explains, in these instances, "you defeat the entire point of the class if you read summaries or skim . . . you just have to do the reading."

Example #2

Here's a slightly more challenging example that comes from the syllabus of a political science course titled Comparative Health Policy.

Lecture #4—The Quest for National Health Insurance: Clinton Health Care Plan

Reading:

Enthoven, Alain. "Managed Competition: An Agenda for Action," *Health Affairs* 7, no. 3 (Summer 1988): 25–47.

Eckholm, Erik. (1993) "Introduction," in *The President's Health Security Plan*. New York: Times Books, vii–xvi. ISBN: 0812923863.

Skocpol, Theda. "The Rise and Demise of the Clinton Health Plan," in *Health Affairs* 14, no. 1 (Spring 1995): 66–85.

Heclo, Hugh. "The Clinton Health Plan: Historical Perspective," in *Health Affairs* 14, no. 1 (Spring 1995): 86–98.

Peterson, Mark A. (1998) "The Politics of Health Care Policy: Overreaching in an Age of Polarization," in Margaret Weir, ed., *The Social Divide*. Washington, D.C.: Brookings Institution Press, 181–229.

What makes this example hard is that the course has no obvious favored sources. That is, there is no textbook or reader that shows up for every class. The key, in this situation, is to use the lecture title as a clue. The rule can be simply stated as follows: **In a course with no fa-**

vored sources, readings that directly address the specific topic of the
lecture act as the favored sources for the day. Treat the rest as supplemental.

In this example, the lecture is titled The Quest for National Health
Insurance: Clinton Health Care Plan. Therefore, the Erik Eckholm,
Hugh Heclo, and Theda Skocpol assignments should become your favored sources, since all three deal directly with the Clinton health
care agenda. You should read these carefully.

The two other articles are supplemental. Because they look like
they contain arguments relevant to the topic of health care under
Clinton, they fall at the top of our supplemental reading importance
hierarchy, and, therefore, they demand enough attention to reveal
their argument. A smart approach would be to read the introductions to both of these articles, and then take careful notes on their
theses.

Confirming Your Decisions

You should always use the lecture itself to confirm your choice
about what to read and what to skip. If the professor emphasizes the
importance of a work that you dismissed (which will happen occasionally—this system isn't perfect), then make a note that you will
need to go back and cover this reading in more detail before the next
exam. A smart technique is to simply write these skipped readings
right onto your syllabus as an assignment for a later class. Choose a
day with a light reading load, and treat the assignment as if it was
given to you by your professor. If you don't explicitly schedule a time
to cover this material, you will invariably procrastinate and then find
yourself with a huge reading list to cover right before the exam.

On the other hand, if you find your professor is discussing certain assignments in a lot of detail, then use this input to scale back how closely you are reading at home. As Lydia from Dartmouth explains: "If you pay close attention in class and take good notes, much of the reading is often unnecessary."

Take Smart Notes on Your Favored Reading Assignments

We've discussed which readings to ignore or skim. But the logical next question is what to do with the favored sources that you decide to read carefully. In this situation, how you take notes on the reading makes a big difference. If you write down very little, the assignment can be completed fast, but the time will be wasted because you won't have bothered to extract the big ideas in a way that makes them accessible when it comes time to study. If, on the other hand, you take detailed notes on every paragraph, your assignments will take way too long to complete. The best compromise is to use a strategy similar to the one outlined earlier for taking lecture notes.

To refresh your memory, the core of this strategy is that all big ideas can be reduced to a *question, evidence*, and *conclusion*. This approach can work wonderfully for reading assignments as well. Apply it as follows:

First, as with lectures, try to take notes on your computer. They will be more organized and easier to follow later on, when you use them for review. In addition, typing makes it easier to record more and finish faster. Next, carefully read the beginning of the assignment. Look for the question being answered by the author. Note that this is different than a thesis statement. For example, "Why did the Clinton health care plan fail?" is a question. "The Clinton health care plan failed because of resistance from commercial health care providers" is a thesis. In a reading assignment, the question can usually be found in the title or perhaps explained in the first few sentences. Record this in your notes, and label it clearly.

Next, look for the author's conclusion (the thesis statement). This is perhaps the most difficult part, since academics are known to propose complicated answers to their questions, especially when writing. So it may take some serious consideration to figure out what's being suggested. Search the first few paragraphs; this is typically where the conclusion is hidden. Also check the final few paragraphs. Often a thesis is proposed at the beginning of an article but then refined slightly at the end once all of the supporting evidence has been presented. When you feel confident in your understanding of the conclusion, record it carefully in your notes. Don't worry if it takes several sentences to capture the point—err on the side of being thorough.

Now comes the easy part: Skim the entire reading. Don't take notes yet. Instead, use a pencil to make checkmarks next to important paragraphs that jump out at you. Because you are reading fast, you may miss some points—don't worry. "Just get the gist of the author's message and how he is supporting that message with evidence, then move on," explains Jason, a straight-A student from the University of Pennsylvania. You don't need to capture everything. Your goal is simply to mark a few solid examples that justify the conclusion as the answer to the question.

Once you have skimmed through the entire reading, go back and find your check marks. For each mark, record in your notes a concise summary of the corresponding point. Label each point in your notes with the page number where you found it. This shouldn't take long. Don't worry about being formal or grammatically correct. Just dump these pieces of evidence into your notes. When you're done, your notes should contain a clearly labeled question followed by a half-dozen or so bullet-pointed pieces of evidence, then a clearly labeled conclusion.

And that's it! A typical article or book chapter should fill, at most, a page of single-spaced notes and take no longer than twenty to thirty minutes to complete. If it takes you longer, then you're likely reading too slowly when you make your check marks. Don't be afraid to move quickly—if you understand the question and the conclusion, all you need is a sampling of the evidence that connects the two. As Matthew from Brown puts it, your goal should be to "read for arguments, not facts."

Don't Work Alone on Problem Sets

Perhaps the most important rule for taming the problem sets assigned in technical courses is to follow our earlier rule and work on them constantly. As Ryan, a straight-A student from Dartmouth, explains: "You can work on problem sets in small pieces while you're between classes or activities." Concentrating on only one or two problems a day will help you avoid mental fatigue. Once your brain gets tired, it's easy to stall—but if you spread out your work, you will end up spending fewer hours on the assignment than if you tried to do it all at once.

Even with a smart schedule, however, you will probably still get stuck occasionally. When this happens, use all the available resources to help you get unstuck. If you're allowed to collaborate with your classmates, which is often the case in technical courses, definitely take advantage of this opportunity. As Greta from Dartmouth explains, working in groups "can drastically cut the time required to finish a really hard problem set." Identify one or two students who share a similar skill level as you and then construct a regular schedule for working together on the class assignments. Set your meeting dates for two or three days before the deadlines; this gives you time to first try the problems on your own and identify the ones that give you the most trouble. Then, when you meet with your problem set group, your energy will be focused where it's needed most. However, don't meet the day before your deadline. It's important to have at least one day before handing in the assignment so you can review all of your answers and fix any small mistakes.

You should also take advantage of office hours. Most technical courses hold office hours once a week, usually run by a teaching assistant (TA). These meetings are meant to clarify complicated concepts from class *and* to be a source of help on hard problems. Always go to office hours, if you have time, and arrive knowing which homework problems pose the biggest challenge to you. Don't be afraid to ask for help. You will learn a lot during these weekly sessions, since the TAs will be able to walk you through the more difficult concepts—which will ultimately save you a lot of time and frustration.

Solve Problems on the Go

Hard problems don't care about your schedule. If you set aside a specific hour to work on a problem set, there is no guarantee that you'll be able to find the answers during this time. This is especially true if the problems you are trying to solve require creative insight, which can't be forced. Sitting and staring at a blank sheet of paper won't always produce results.

Working with a group can help you bypass these mental blocks. But often, group work is most useful when you've already thought of potential solutions for most of the problems. It would be too time consuming to try to solve *all* of the problems from scratch with a group. With this in mind, you need a solid strategy for solving problems on your own without busting your schedule. A smart technique, used by many talented technical students, is to solve problems on the go. Here's how it works:

First, set aside a little block of time to familiarize yourself with a couple of problems, and make sure you understand exactly what is being asked. You may need to review your notes to refamiliarize yourself with the relevant concepts.

Next, try to solve the problem in the most obvious way possible. This, of course, probably won't work, because most difficult problems are tricky by nature. By failing in this initial approach, however, you will have at least identified *what* makes this problem hard. Now you are ready to try to come up with a real solution.

The next step is counterintuitive. After you've primed the problem, put away your notes and move on to something else. Instead of trying to force a solution, think about the problem in between other activities. As you walk across campus, wait in line at the dining hall, or take a shower, bring up the problem in your head and start thinking through solutions. You might even want to go on a quiet hike or long car ride dedicated entirely to mulling over the question at hand.

More often than not, after enough mobile consideration, you will finally stumble across a solution. Only then should you schedule more time to go back to the problem set, write it down formally, and work out the kinks. It's unclear exactly *why* solving problems is easier when you're on the go, but, whatever the explanation, it has worked for many students. Even better, it saves a lot of time, since most of your thinking has been done in little interludes between other activities, not during big blocks of valuable free time.

Write Solutions Right the First Time

Another important time-saving tip for problem set work is to record solutions formally the first time you write them down. Many students first jot down their answers informally and then return later to reformat them into something neat enough for submission. There is no reason to include both steps. You are, for no good reason, adding a lot of extra time to the process. Instead, go slowly and deliberately the first time. Write your answer carefully, and clean it up immediately until it is of submission quality. Then you can cross the assignment off your list and it will be one less thing to worry about.

Step 3

Marshal Your Resources

Here's a surprising fact: Most straight-A students don't think "studying" is a big deal. They realize that the bulk of the work required to ace an exam has already been accomplished through identifying big ideas in lectures, extracting arguments from reading assignments, and solving problem sets. By the time the test date rolls around, all that's left is a targeted review of the ideas that they have already mastered and internalized. Students who pull sleepless study marathons, on the other hand, are spending most of their time trying to learn from scratch the ideas that they could have been internalizing, bit by bit, as the term progressed. So forget the conventional wisdom that more studying equals better grades. Smart students understand that **if you're studying hard, then you've done something wrong.** Preparing for a test should not be painful. And it should not require a lot of time.

If you have been putting Steps #1 and #2 into practice, taking smart notes and handling assignments effectively, studying should not be a big deal for you either. In fact, when faced with a looming quiz or exam, you have to do only two things. First, organize your material intelligently. Second, perform a targeted review of this material. This section will teach you how to accomplish the former. Don't worry—organizing your material properly is not a difficult task, but it is important that you do it right. Many students neglect this step, eager to dive right into the review, but by doing so they condemn themselves to hours of unnecessary work. You don't want to be like these students. Pay attention to the advice that follows and you will experience a significant reduction to the difficulty of your study experience.

Define the Challenge

Before you can conduct any meaningful studying, you must first define the scope of the exam. As Simon from Brown puts it: "You need to know what kind of information the professor wants you to know." To accomplish this goal, answer the following questions:

- Which lectures and reading assignments (or problem sets) are fair game?

- What type of questions will there be, and how many of each? As Christine from Harvard explains: "It's helpful to know in advance what *kind* of knowledge will be asked for on the exam—IDs, dates, broad syntheses of the texts' major arguments?"

- Is the exam open note or open book?

- For a technical class, will formulas be provided or do they need to be memorized?

- How much time will be available? Does the professor expect the exam to be easy to complete during the test period or a challenge?

Some professors offer answers to these questions without being prompted. Many, however, do not. If it's two weeks before the exam, and the professor hasn't mentioned any details yet, you should ask. If you're shy, ask after class. But get the information as early as possible—it's crucial to your success.

Build a Study Guide (*Organizing Nontechnical Course Material*)

"I have always been a big fan of making a study guide," admits Ryan from Dartmouth. This is a technique that popped up again and again in my straight-A interviews. Each student, of course, had his or her own variation on study guide creation, but they all followed, more or less, this same general approach:

For a nontechnical course, once you find out which lectures and reading assignments are fair game for the exam, print out the corresponding notes that you've typed up or gather the pages you've written on (don't be afraid to deconstruct your notebook). Cluster these pages into piles, separated by general topic. Clearly label each of these piles with its topic and fasten them together with a paper clip so you can easily transport them without mixing up the pages. This final step is important, since you will be moving to and from your various isolated study spaces once you begin your review. For simplicity, we will refer to these topic-themed piles as "chapters." Your final study guide, therefore, should contain a chapter, consisting of reading and lecture notes, for each general topic that might be covered on the exam.

Construct a Mega-Problem Set
(*Organizing Technical Course Material*)

For a technical course, many students follow a variant of the study guide approach that focuses on sample problems. It works as follows:

Your problem set assignments are the key to your review process. Start a pile for each problem set that covers material that might appear on the exam. Next, you'll need to supplement each problem set with sample problems from your lecture notes. For each lecture relevant to the upcoming exam, do the following:

1. Match the lecture to the problem set that covers the same material.

2. Copy sample problems from these lecture notes onto a blank sheet of paper. You don't have to copy the steps or the answers, just the questions.

3. Label the blank sheet of paper with the date of the lecture. This will help you later figure out where these problems came

from (and more important, where their answers can be found).

4. Fasten this sheet with a paper clip to the problem set you matched it to in step one.

In other words, this process transforms your problem sets into *mega-problem sets* by adding extra problems drawn from your lecture notes. Pretty simple.

Finally, you must augment your mega-problem sets with *technical explanation questions*. What are these? For every major topic covered in a particular mega-problem set, jot down a question that asks you to explain the basics of the topic. For example, as Greta from Dartmouth recounts, in an "economics course, I would make study sheets and then add a general question such as: *what happens when a government increases spending and lowers interest rates?*" Or, for a chemistry class, you might have a problem set containing many questions that require you to draw the molecular structure of specific chemical compounds. In this case, you could add a technical explanation question along the lines of: "Explain the general procedure for drawing a molecular structure, why this is useful, and what special cases must be kept in mind."

It's important that you add these technical explanation questions in addition to your regular sample problems, since they will reveal whether or not you understand the underlying concepts or if you've just memorized the steps for some particular problems.

One last note: If your professor makes a practice exam available, then print out a copy of it and store it with your mega-problem sets. For technical courses, sample exams are a great review tool, and you will definitely want to have them handy when it comes time to study.

Prepare Memorization Aids

Both technical and nontechnical courses sometimes require you to do some memorization—formulas, chemical equations, artwork, dates, or chronologies—and the most efficient way to memorize this information is by using flash cards. Almost every straight-A student interviewed for this book used flash cards to help with rote memorization. Fortunately, this technique is easy. Buy a stack of index cards, put the prompt on one side and the answer on the other. Constructing these flash cards, however, can take longer than you might imagine, so start early. If possible, start writing up your cards at least a week before the first day you plan to actually study. The activity is mindless—you can write flash cards while watching TV—so it shouldn't be too hard to get them done, in advance, bit by bit.

Schedule Your Organization Wisely

Don't try to organize and study in the same day. This is a crucial tactic used by many straight-A students. When you review, you want your brain at full power. If you organize your materials the same day that you review them, your brain will be too tired to accomplish both effectively. So keep these two tasks separate and you'll end up working more effectively, which reduces the total time spent and produces better results.

Step 4

Conquer the Material

Now it's time to get down to business. For weeks, you've taken smart notes and extracted insights from your assignments. You've identified the scope of the exam and organized all the relevant information into study guides or mega-problem sets. Your flash cards are stacked and ready to go. You're rested. Your time has come. There is nothing left to do but, dare we say it, *study*.

This is the step students most commonly identify with exam preparation. It's also the step that most students misguidedly spend the majority of their time on. You're not most students—at least not anymore. All of the work you put in up to this point was meant to make this one step as small and painless and insignificant as possible. So don't worry. There are no all-nighters in your future.

What follows are powerful techniques for taking your imposing piles of study material and imprinting the key ideas on your mind as efficiently as possible. These techniques are quick but ruthlessly effective. Use them with confidence. They get the job done, and they get it done fast.

Trust the Quiz-and-Recall Method

Whether it's philosophy or calculus, the most effective way to imprint a concept is to first review it and then try to explain it, unaided, in your own words. If you can close your eyes and articulate an argument from scratch, or stare at a blank sheet of paper and reproduce a solution without a mistake, then you have fully imprinted that concept. It's not going anywhere.

The same is *not* true if you merely read over something. Passively reviewing a concept is not the same as actively producing it. Most students make the mistake of relying only on passive review; they read and reread their notes and assignments, and assume that the more they read, the more they will remember. But as Ryan from Dartmouth warns: "Simply reading it over doesn't work. You have to make the extra effort to get it into your head."

Using the Quiz-and-Recall Method for Nontechnical Courses

To apply the quiz-and-recall method to nontechnical course material, you first need to construct a practice quiz for each chapter in your study guide. Fortunately, the questions for these quizzes already exist, since, if you've followed the advice of Steps #1 and #2, all of your notes should be in a question/evidence/conclusion format. There-fore, the quiz for any given chapter can simply contain all of the questions from the notes you took for that chapter. You can be flexible here. If your notes contain some really broad questions—for example, an entire lecture that deals with only one idea—break them up into several smaller questions that, together, cover all of the relevant points. On the other hand, if your notes have a bunch of really small questions, you can combine some into larger questions to save space and time. This process is not an exact science; your goal is simply to produce practice quizzes that cover all the material contained in each corresponding chapter. If you can answer all the questions, then you understand all the big ideas.

Once you've built your practice quizzes, go through them one by one. For each question, try to articulate the matching conclusion and provide some highlights from the supporting evidence. You don't have to reproduce the material in your notes word for word, but you do need a reasonable summary of the big idea and its support.

Here's the important part: ***Don't do this only in your head!*** If you're in a private location, say your answers out loud using complete sentences. As Lydia from Dartmouth explains: "I find that walking around and saying things out loud commits them to memory in a spectacular way." If it helps, act as if you're giving a lecture on the subject. Follow Lydia's suggestion and pace around while providing your answer. Get your blood pumping. Put some music on in the background. Make it an event. Your study guide was designed to be portable, so it shouldn't be too difficult to find a place to be alone. For this crucial step, think beyond the library. I used to do this type of review while walking a nature trail on campus. One of the students I interviewed reviews on the treadmill. Be creative. Studying doesn't have to involve long hours sitting at a desk.

However, if you are forced to review with other people around and you need to be quiet, then you can write out your answers. "The physical act of writing and the manipulation of the material in my mind was usually enough to keep things straight," explains Melanie, a straight-A Dartmouth student. You don't have to format these responses perfectly with correct spelling and grammar, but they must contain all of the pertinent information. No shortcuts. If you don't say or write it, don't consider it fully reviewed.

Next, put little check marks on your quizzes next to any questions that you had trouble answering. Glance through your study guide to remind yourself of the right answers to these questions. Take a quick break.

Now, repeat the first step, except this time you need to answer only the questions that you marked during your first run-through. Put a new check mark next to the questions that you still have trouble with. Once again, look through your notes to get the right answers, and then take a quick break. Then go back to the practice quiz and try to answer the questions that you marked on your second run-through. You get the idea.

Repeat this pattern until you complete a run-through without adding any new check marks. At this point, you're done!

The power of this approach is its efficiency. You spend the least amount of time with the questions that you understand the best, and you spend the most amount of time with the questions that cause you the most trouble. You also have a definite endpoint. There is no need to wonder how much longer you should continue reviewing. Once you finish a round without any more check marks, you're finished, and not a minute is wasted.

Many students are uneasy with how little time is required by this process. They feel like they should continue to review their quizzes, again and again, up until the moment of the exam. This is unnecessary! The quiz-and-recall method is powerful because it does not depend on multiple reviews of the same information. Once you've articulated an answer out loud in complete sentences, or recorded it clearly with pencil and paper, it will stick in your mind. As Chris from Dartmouth explains: "[The quiz-and-recall method] takes much less time than people think it does—one day to make the quizzes for the term, and only a few hours to review."

Using the Quiz-and-Recall Method for Technical Courses

The quiz-and-recall method is easily applied to technical courses. You already constructed your mega-problem sets; now you simply need to solve them. Start with the technical explanation questions—thinking about the general concepts first will make it easier to solve the specific sample problems that follow. As with nontechnical courses, try to provide an articulate answer for each problem, and if possible, give your explanation out loud, as if lecturing to a class. Otherwise, write out your answers clearly. Don't skip any important details.

Once you're done with the technical explanation questions, move on to the sample problems. Try to answer each. Again, **don't do this in your head**. "I don't just read the material," explains Worasom, a straight-A student from Brown. "I write the important equations and concepts out by hand." Your solutions don't need to be as detailed as if this was a real assignment, but they should clearly demonstrate that you know what you're doing. If you can't explain exactly how you got from the question to the answer, then you don't yet understand this problem. Be honest with yourself: If you're just regurgitating memorized solutions, you aren't prepared to handle new questions on a test.

As before, check mark the questions that give you trouble. Review the solutions for these questions. Take a break. Then repeat the process, except this time try to answer only the questions you marked on the previous pass. Follow this method until you finish a round with no checked problems. When this happens, you're done.

Doris from Harvard explains a final caveat for technical course preparation: "If professors make exams from past years available, these are a terrific resource." In this case, wait until after you finish your quiz-and-recall, and then try to complete the exam under timed test-taking conditions. Consider this a final check that you understand all of the needed concepts. If you have trouble with a few questions on this practice exam, review them carefully. If you have trouble with a lot of questions on this practice exam, then something went wrong with your previous review, and you need to go back through the material. Work through another round of question answering, and this time really make sure you understand each of the steps. If you still have trouble, then it's time to seek out help from a classmate or a TA.

Memorize over Time

If you have material that must be truly memorized—dates, artists, chronologies, formulas—there are, unfortunately, no real shortcuts. You just have to keep working with your flash cards until you have no trouble providing the right answer, even after you shuffle the cards into a random order.

Memorization is particularly dependent on your available mental energy. It doesn't work if you try to commit items to memory for eight hours straight, but it does work if you memorize only an hour at a time and only one or two hours a day. So separate the task of memorizing from your other review. Spread the work out over many days, and never dedicate too much time to any one sitting with your flash cards. Melanie from Dartmouth recalls how some of her peers would "review their flash cards at any opportunity—eating dinner, waiting in line at an e-mail terminal," which is the most effective way to get through this tedious task and commit the necessary items to memory.

Step 5

Invest in "Academic Disaster Insurance"

Most college students have an exam horror story to tell. These stories always seem to start the same way. The first question on the test is easily solved, you still have plenty of time, and everything feels good. Then you see it—a question that you have no idea how to answer. Leaving it blank will torpedo your grade, and as you sit and stare, the time to solve the other questions quietly slips away. The good feeling is gone, and in its place, panic creeps in. You've just experienced an academic disaster.

Conventional wisdom says that academic disasters are unavoidable. No one can study every single topic, and therefore you are going to get nailed occasionally. But here's the lesson of Step #5: *Don't believe this*.

Straight-A students have a knack for avoiding rogue questions. It's as if they invest in some sort of academic disaster insurance: protection against the unexpected return of those obscure topics that slip by when you doze off for a moment in class. In reality, this insurance policy is nothing more than a simple strategy: *Eliminate your question marks*. This technique can be employed throughout the term and, over time, significantly reduce the chance that you will be baffled by an unexpected exam question.

Eliminate Your Question Marks

In Step #1, we covered smart techniques for taking notes in class. If you remember, this strategy suggests that you put a question mark in your notes for any topic that flies by without you really understanding the conclusion. This will occur occasionally in both technical and nontechnical courses—sometimes as the result of your attention wandering and sometimes as the result of the professor heading off on a tangent and not offering a satisfactory explanation.

These question marks are dangerous. As Christine from Harvard puts it, by skipping a point made in a lecture, "you're gambling with the possibility of being truly in the dark on the exam." The scenario is simple. During the semester a few topics slip past your attention in class, so you end up with a handful of question marks in your notes. When it comes time to study, you have more than enough big ideas that you do understand, and that you need to review, so the occasional question-marked topic gets ignored. You enter the exam feeling prepared, and then, as luck would have it, you find yourself face-to-face with a big essay question covering one of those bypassed concepts. *Whoops.*

To prevent this from happening, you need to eliminate these question marks. **The key is to start this process well before the exam.** If you leave all of these question marks unanswered until you start studying, you will end up spending many extra hours looking up the required explanations. Learning a large quantity of material from scratch during the review process is a mistake made by average students—and you should avoid this.

Instead, try to knock off question marks as soon as they arrive. By the time you begin studying you should, as Robert, a straight-A student from Brown, explains, "have at least a vague understanding of every topic that will be covered on the exam." The following four tactics, if used regularly, will help you achieve this goal. They provide a solid defense against unclear ideas and will allow you to start the study process with an explanation in mind for *all* relevant topics.

- **Ask questions during class.**

  "When in doubt, I just ask questions in class for more clarification," explains Worasom from Brown. If a topic slides by you, raise your hand and ask for a clarification. The more question marks you eliminate on the spot, the less work you will have to do later.

- **Develop the habit of talking to your professor briefly after class.**

  "Talk to the professor after class, or send him an e-mail asking for clarification about questions that arose during his lecture," suggests Jason from Penn. There is nothing unusual about this. Most professors will stick around for five or ten minutes after the bell to answer final questions. Take advantage of this time. When the class ends, head over to the professor and see how many of the question marks of the day you can get eliminated. You should then immediately correct your notes before you forget the explanations. Will this turn you into a brownnoser? *No!* The brownnosers are those who come up to the professor only to tell him what parts of the lecture they found interesting, or to offer up some of their own "brilliant" thoughts on the topic. You, on the other hand, have a list of focused questions that you want answered, which makes you seem smart, not sniveling.

- **Ask classmates.**
  If you're still unclear, James, a straight-A student from Dartmouth, recommends that you "talk with other people about the topic." Send an e-mail or corner them in the hall soon after the lecture. If they understand the topic, it will take them only a few minutes to explain it to you while it's still fresh in their minds.

- **Come prepared to exam review sessions (if offered).**
  Many classes offer a formal review session the week before the exam. Go to these. Before you arrive, jot down all of the topics from your notes that you are still unsure about. Then, during the session, try to get all of them answered. Don't be worried about having a lot to discuss. More often than not, review sessions suffer from too *few* student questions, so your professor or TA will appreciate your preparation.

The goal of these defensive tactics is to eliminate your question marks without adding any study time. If, however, despite your best attempts, some of these unclear topics persist until your review, your last-ditch defense is to skim. You probably won't have time at this point to look up detailed explanations from scratch for every leftover question mark. And, even if you did, the effort would be way too time consuming (remember: Straight-A students avoid long study hours), so skim over just enough material to have *something* to say for each of these points. On the off chance that one of these lingering question-marked topics comes up on the exam, at least you won't leave a blank page. But this situation can still be dangerous, so follow the first four strategies to reduce the topics you don't understand as much as possible before your studying begins.

Step 6

Provide "A+" Answers

The final step of the straight-A process is actually taking the test. Many students incorrectly believe that preparation is the only thing that counts. To them, taking a test is a simple matter of showing off what they know. This type of thinking is risky. Why? *Even the most prepared student can bomb an exam due to poor test-taking skills.*

The potential pitfalls during an exam are numerous, but the most common are: (1) running out of time and (2) providing answers that, although detailed, don't fully answer all parts of the question being asked. In fact, these two dangers work together in a devilish counterbalance, making them particularly hard to conquer. That is, if you try to avoid spending too much time on questions, then you are likely to provide incomplete answers. On the other hand, if you try to provide detailed answers, then you are likely to run out of time.

The situation sounds dire, but it's not. With the right strategy, you can eliminate these fears and ensure that your grade properly reflects your level of preparation. Straight-A students recognize this point, and when asked about test-taking, they provided detailed responses, proving that for them, this final step is no mere afterthought. They treat the test-taking process with great respect, and this attention is reflected in their consistently high grades.

Their advice has been culled into five key strategies. Together, they provide a comprehensive test-taking system, finely tuned through experience to maximize performance. Follow these rules on every exam, and you'll be able to transform yourself into a test-taking machine—cool, confident, and ruthlessly efficient as you move from question to question, providing the best possible answers.

Strategy #1: Review First, Answer Questions Later

"I always read through the entire exam first," explains Robert from Brown. This is good advice—for any exam, your first step should always be to review all of the questions. If it's an essay exam or a technical exam with a relatively small number of questions, then read each prompt carefully. If the exam is multiple choice or contains many questions, skim through quickly and get a feel for which topics are covered.

This review familiarizes you with the length and relative difficulty of what lies ahead. It also primes your brain for the topics you'll need to address. "Always scan all the questions," explains Anna from Dartmouth. "This allows your mind to think about all of them, even while you are focusing on one in particular." In other words, while you toil away on an early question, another part of your brain, working in the background, will begin to retrieve information relating to the topics still to come. This actually happens, and it helps you answer the later questions more quickly.

Finally, and perhaps most significantly, this first step also helps you relax. Stress proliferates in a classroom right before an exam is distributed. It's a make-or-break situation. Months of effort have led up to this single moment, and you have only a scant hour or two to prove what you know and secure your final grade. You begin to question yourself. Did you study everything you needed to? Have you forgotten important ideas? What if the exam focuses on a subject you know nothing about? If you left it blank, what would happen then? Just thinking about this situation is enough to make most undergrads sweat.

However, by taking the first few minutes to carefully review the exam, you break this mounting tension. It gives you something productive to do that doesn't involve actually answering questions. Once you complete this task and build a better idea of what to expect, the exam becomes less menacing. You've seen the questions, and (hopefully) none seem impossible. You begin to say to yourself: *Okay, maybe this isn't all that bad*. Your confidence rises, your heart rate lowers, and your stress begins to dissipate. Now you can turn your full attention to providing standout responses.

Strategy #2: Build a Time Budget

At any given point during an exam, you should know the maximum number of minutes you have to spend on the current question before moving on to the next. As Doris from Harvard puts it: "I lay down very strict time limits for myself on each question." This strategy goes a long way toward avoiding time trouble; it keeps your attention focused and prevents you from spending too much time on any particular question.

The key to maintaining this keen awareness is to build a time budget. First, take the time allotted for the exam and subtract ten minutes. Next, divide this amount by the number of questions. The result is how long you have to spend on each prompt.

What should you do with this information? For an exam with a small number of questions, mark right on the test pages the time when you should begin and finish each one. For an exam with many questions, divide the exam into equal fourths, then jot down the time you should begin and end each section. In both cases, these recorded times will keep you updated on how close your current progress matches your predetermined schedule.

Why do we subtract ten minutes in the first step? This provides a safety buffer. You want a few extra minutes available here and there to be able to double check your answers when you are finished, or go back and add more insights to questions on which you were rushed.

Strategy #3: Proceed from Easy to Hard

Straight-A students almost never answer exam questions in the order that they are presented. Years of informal experimentation by successful students have demonstrated that the most effective way to tackle an exam is to answer the easiest questions first, and this is exactly what you should do. Start with the most approachable questions before moving on to the more forbidding. Don't worry if this has you skipping around all over the exam—in most cases the provided order is irrelevant.

The advantage of this approach is that it first focuses your energy on the questions you know the most about, ensuring that you get maximum points on these. It also gives you a better chance of conquering the more difficult ones. "I always skip a question if it does not come to me immediately," explains Ryan from Dartmouth. "This keeps my mind clear to answer other questions and hopefully something will jog my memory."

When you come across something hard early on in the exam, your natural instinct is to panic. You have so many more questions to finish, and you can almost feel the minutes ticking away as you stare blankly at this one particular roadblock. It can be tough to get your focus back to wring out as many points as possible from the easier questions that follow.

If, instead, you tackle this same roadblock at the end of the exam, you'll find that the situation seems less dire. You've answered everything else, so all that's left to do is working out this final puzzler. More often than not, you will find the mental block diminished. Without the pressure of other questions looming in the background, you can take a more relaxed approach. You might not know the *best* answer, but you can spend some time to devise a *reasonable* answer. Because you have nothing else left to finish, you can spend the remainder of the time polishing this answer, thinking, and repolishing. The result is the strongest possible outcome given your state of preparation.

Strategy #4: Outline Essays

When facing an essay question, don't just start writing and see what happens. This approach leads to rambling answers and missed concepts. Instead, your first step should be to jot down a quick outline. This might seem like a waste of time, but in truth it can be invaluable.

First, reread the question carefully. As Matthew from Brown explains: "Usually, you can isolate three or four mini-questions from a single essay question." Underline each of these mini-questions; this will help you flesh out your outline and avoid an incomplete answer. "Then, outline on paper (not in your head) the way that you will use what you know to answer these mini-questions," continues Matthew. To do so, use the margin of the exam to jot down all of the points you can recall that are relevant to the question. Record only a few key words for each point to save time and space. For example, if you want to mention an argument made by an author named Robert Caro dealing with Lyndon Johnson's views on race relations, you might jot down: "Caro—race."

Next, go back and check the question parts you underlined in the first step. Make sure each is adequately addressed by the points you just noted in the margin. When you're sure that you have identified all the relevant information for the essay, number these points in the order that you want to present them.

Only now should you begin writing your essay. Follow your outline, and the writing will proceed smoothly. You should be able to quickly produce a solid response that draws on everything you reviewed and addresses all parts of the question asked.

Strategy #5: Check Your Work

"At the end," explains Chris from Dartmouth, "I always check my answers." If you have extra time at the end of the exam (may you be so lucky), then follow Chris's advice and go back and check your work. You will be surprised by how many times this final review turns up a mistake in a technical problem or an important concept that you forgot to mention in an essay.

If, after your first round of review, you still have time left over, then go through and check again. If there is a problem you feel particularly shaky on, use this time to go over it in detail, augmenting the answer wherever appropriate. Don't worry about using carets and arrows to add in new phrases and facts to your essays, or to point out added steps in your technical problems. Neatness doesn't count on exams; it's the content that matters.

It's tempting to relax after finishing your exam, perhaps walking proudly to the front of the classroom and handing it in before anyone else. But aside from the wistful stares of your classmates, this strategy is ill conceived. Double checking your work up to the last minute can make the difference between an above-average student and an academic star.

The Plan in Action

Now let's look at how the steps for Part Two play out in the real world. This section presents two realistic case studies, both demonstrating how a hypothetical student uses straight-A strategies to prepare for an exam. You'll notice that each student has a couple of curveballs thrown into the mix. For example, Julie has a big paper due the same Monday as her midterm, so she can't simply cram all weekend. And Michael doesn't even start his review until a couple of days before the exam.

The key here is to notice the flexibility with which these students apply the advice. This underscores the main lesson of these case studies: *A study system is only as useful as your ability to adapt it to your unique situation.* Both of our students manage to fit their review into an already busy schedule and do so without ever cramming, pulling all-nighters, or even spending more than a few hours studying on any given day.

Case Study #1—Julie's History Midterm

The final grade for Julie's history class is based only on a midterm, a final, and one paper. Therefore, her performance on this upcoming midterm is important. The following timeline of Julie's preparation will give you a feel for how she spreads out the necessary work for optimal results.

Monday—Two Weeks Before the Midterm

At the beginning of class, the professor issues a quick reminder about the upcoming exam. Taking advantage of the situation, Julie raises her hand to ask what it will cover and in what format. The professor offers the following information:

- The exam will consist mainly of essay questions. The topics will be broad, but the student will need to draw support from the reading assignments.

- There will also be a timeline section that will present a group of historical events covered in the class and then ask the student to rearrange them into chronological order.

Now that Julie has a better feel for what to expect, she can construct a rough study schedule. Her biggest problem is that she has a big paper due for another class on the same day as the midterm! This prevents her from using the weekend before the exam as a big cram

session (the strategy used by most students). She's going have to figure out a way to tackle her preparation in advance.

Julie decides that she will start her review this upcoming weekend
(a little more than a week before the exam). Specifically, she will use
this weekend to organize the necessary materials, which shouldn't
take long. She will then use the week that follows to actually do the
review, spreading the work out into little chunks so she won't get behind in her other obligations. That's all the time that she can spare.
In particular, notice that she hasn't scheduled any studying for the
Saturday and Sunday right before the big exam—she expects this
time to be consumed with paper writing.

To implement this plan, she follows the advice of Part One and
records the details on her calendar, writing on each day what work
she should accomplish. This will save her a lot of stress—most students spend the week or so before an exam constantly worried about
whether they should be studying and whether they have enough
time left to prepare. Julie, on the other hand, is free from these wor-
ries. All she has to do is look at her calendar each morning and schedule a time for whatever piece of the study process she finds recorded
for the day.

Saturday—Nine Days Before the Midterm

Julie's busy. As on most weekends, she has a lot of schoolwork to
finish for Monday, and she also has some ambitious social plans for
the evening, so her time is certainly limited.

The goal of this weekend is to organize her history materials,
which thankfully doesn't demand a lot of hard thinking. (Julie hopes
to get *some* relaxation out of her two days off.) She consults her cal-

endar: Today (Saturday), she should print hard copies of all the relevant notes and then prepare the memorization aids for the timeline section. Tomorrow (Sunday), she will focus her energy on constructing the practice quizzes for her notes.

First, Julie sets aside an hour before lunch to print out the lecture and reading notes she made during the first half of class. She gathers the printouts, stashes them in a folder, then she heads off to meet some friends for lunch.

Later that afternoon, she sets aside another half hour to work on her memorization aids. Fortunately, all of the major events discussed in the lectures were also described in the class textbook. Though most of these events were covered in much more detail in the other reading assignments, to construct a simple list of events (and their respective dates) requires only a quick scan through of this one book. As she comes across each relevant event, she jots the name on one side of an index card, and then puts the date on the other side.

Sunday—Eight Days Before the Midterm

Midmorning, a slightly groggy Julie (it was an eventful Saturday night) pulls herself out of bed, snags her laptop, her folder of note printouts, and a large coffee, and then heads to one of her favorite secret study spots. Being early on a Sunday (at least, early relative to the typical college student schedule), the library is deserted—just the way she likes it.

Getting down to business, Julie first sorts her notes into piles by subject. Some notes, of course, seem to straddle multiple subjects. That's okay. The piles are just a rough form of organization. Nothing has to be exact here. She ends up with six piles, which together constitute her study guide for the midterm.

Julie then goes through each printout in her first pile, typing quiz questions on her laptop as she proceeds. Sometimes she copies questions straight off her notes. Other times she puts down a more general question that covers several smaller points described in her notes. It doesn't really matter exactly how she chooses the quiz questions, just as long as the questions being typed into her laptop more or less cover every important point discussed in the notes. After about an hour and a half, Julie has finished typing up quizzes for the first three of her six piles.

She breaks for lunch, then returns later in the afternoon and spends another two hours constructing her quizzes. Once she's done, she prints out all six and attaches them to their corresponding piles.

Though Julie's goal for the day was only to organize, the very act of constructing these quizzes has forced her to do a quick review of all the relevant course material—an important first step in internalizing all the necessary information.

Monday Through Friday—The Week Before the Midterm

On Monday, as dictated by her calendar, Julie spends two hours mastering the first two quizzes, a task she accomplishes by pacing around her dorm room and lecturing answers to an imaginary class. (Needless to say, Julie waited for a time when her roommate was out before starting this vocal review.) On Tuesday, she works with her memorization flash cards for forty-five minutes. On Wednesday, she spends two hours mastering the middle two quizzes. On Thursday, she spends another hour with her memorization flash cards. And on Friday, she spends two hours mastering the final two quizzes.

As one might expect, even though she had previously eliminated most question marks in her notes by following the advice of Step #5

(Invest in Academic Disaster Insurance), Julie comes across a handful of questions that she still doesn't really have a satisfactory answer for. She jots down these questionable topics, vowing to deal with them later.

Saturday—Two Days Before the Midterm

Julie had hoped to finish studying before this weekend, but she was busier than she had expected the previous week, so she still has a little more to review. Because she also has a paper deadline on Monday, she knows that, at most, she can spare maybe an hour today for exam preparation. She uses this hour to finish her academic disaster insurance investment; specifically, she takes the list of questions for which she doesn't have great answers and sends e-mails to classmates in hopes of soliciting better ones.

By the end of the day, she has received responses, of varying levels of detail, for most of her outstanding questions. She doesn't feel great about her knowledge on these few points, but at least now she has something to say if it comes down to it.

Monday—The Day of the Midterm

Notice that while most of her classmates sacrificed the entire weekend studying, Julie did little more than send a few e-mails over the last couple of days, leaving her free to focus on her paper. Now that it's the day of the midterm, she still doesn't have much serious preparation pending. During the morning, she shuffles through her memorization flash cards a couple of times and dips into her quizzes at random, answering a half-dozen questions just to boost her confidence. She's rested and ready to go.

Finally, it's time for the exam, and Julie knows exactly what to do. First, she zips right to the chronology section and makes quick work of the listed events. Her flash cards prepared her well. Then, she reviews the four essay questions that follow. She constructs a time budget and tackles the questions in order of difficulty. Her quizzes set her up well to provide thorough, standout answers without too much wasted time thinking about what to say next. She is able to draw from several sources for each question, and because the information is so ingrained in her mind from her earlier quiz-and-recall sessions, she often finds herself being able to recall arguments almost word-for-word from her notes. And because she outlines her essays, she provides answers that pull in as much relevant information as possible and cover all pieces of the topic at hand.

The Aftermath

Julie nailed the chronology section and provided detailed and complete answers to each essay question. Obviously, she gets an A. And this doesn't at all surprise her. Later, when her friends, griping about their B exams, complain about how they spent all weekend "studying," Julie kindly neglects to mention that she studied a grand total of one hour over the weekend and no more than a few hours on any given day before that.

Case Study #2—Michael's Calculus Exam

Michael's taking a calculus class and, as he's quick to admit, he doesn't like calculus. But, as is the case at most colleges, a semester of calculus is required, so Michael's out of luck. The grade for this particular course is based on three exams and a bunch of problem sets. Let's see how Michael uses our system to overcome his lack of a natural affinity for the mathematical arts and pull off a strong grade without too much suffering.

Monday—Four Days Before the First Exam

Yes, Michael's first calculus exam is less than a week away. By this point, as you'll recall, Julie was already well along in her preparation. But there are three things to remember here. One, this exam is not quite as big and as important as Julie's midterm. It covers only a third of the material, and its contribution to Michael's final grade is shared with two other tests and many problem sets. Second, sometimes (okay, many times) people have been known to allow exam dates to slip up on them. If you follow the advice from Part One, this should not happen to you often. But it's important to see how the straight-A system can be adapted and applied even under these tight constraints. Finally, remember that Julie's exam date fell on the same day as a paper was due, so she had to be more conscientious with how she spread out her work.

Because math professors tend to be precise, Michael doesn't need to ask about what the exam will cover. This information is spelled out in the syllabus. Specifically, the exam will draw from all material covered up until last Friday, which was when the professor handed back their last problem set.

As you might imagine, Michael is somewhat stressed about the proximity of the exam. But this stress is mitigated significantly by his knowledge of our system. He knows that his next step is to marshal his resources, and that is what he is going to do tonight. Here's how he proceeds:

The upcoming exam covers the first four weeks of the course. Because Michael had one problem set assigned each week, he now has four graded problem sets to use as the foundations for his mega-problem sets. His first step is to extract sample problems from his notes to add to his existing graded problem sets. Following the strategy of Step #3, he grabs a blank sheet of paper for each of the four weeks of class. He then flips through his notebook and jots down sample problems from his notes onto the appropriate week's sheet of paper. Note: Michael is careful to label each question with the date of the lecture where he found it. This will make it easy to look up the answers in his notebook when it comes time to review. Finally, he attaches each sheet to the corresponding problem set.

When he's done, Michael has four mega-problem sets, each consisting of one graded problem set assignment from class, and a sheet of paper filled with sample problems from his notes.

His final act of organization is to think up some technical discussion questions. For example, during the first week, Michael's class focused on single variable derivatives, so he jots down the following general question on his first mega-problem set: *"Explain what a derivative is, what it describes, and the general procedure for calculating one when given a function."*

Remember, these general explanation questions are crucial. Without them, you run the danger of memorizing specific problems but not learning the technique behind the problems, ill equipping you to handle the fresh problems you will face on the exam.

Because he only has to cover four weeks of material, this process only takes about an hour to complete. Following our prohibition against organizing and reviewing on the same day, Michael calls it quits until tomorrow.

Tuesday—Three Days Before the Exam

Michael's first class is at 11 A.M., so he drags himself out of bed at 8:30 A.M. to put in two hours of studying before his day really gets started. This is especially important because he has a busy afternoon and evening planned, and he is worried that he won't have any other free time to study today. He also believes in our philosophy of trying to finish as much work as possible as early as possible, so this decision comes naturally.

By 9 A.M., Michael has settled into one of his favorite secluded study spots—a deserted upper floor of a small engineering library. He has a bowl of oatmeal in his stomach and a cup of coffee at his side, so you better believe that he's ready to work.

It's time to start the quiz-and-recall process. Michael tries to provide answers for each of the questions contained in his first mega-problem set. He uses a sheet of scratch paper and forces himself to jot down the important steps to each problem. For the technical explanation questions, he actually paces up and down the stacks, lecturing about the topics under his breath. After his first pass-through he takes a ten-minute break, then returns to tackle only the questions that gave him trouble. He continues until he has successfully answered every question. Because he is using the quiz-and-recall method, his focus is directed efficiently. He spends the most time this morning on the problems with which he has the most trouble and the least time on the problems he understands well.

Wednesday—Two Days Before the Exam

The exam looms two days in the future, and Michael has three more weeks' worth of material to master. Realizing the potential urgency of this situation, he carves out two separate two-hour chunks of study for the day, giving him four total hours in which to work. The first chunk is in the morning, the second in the afternoon. The break in between will help Michael's brain recharge and prevent this task from becoming too mentally draining.

As before, it takes Michael most of the first two hours to get through his second mega-problem set. Once again, several passes were required, each one focusing on fewer and fewer problems.

That afternoon, Michael knocks off the third mega-problem set during his second two-hour block. In fact, because this material is more recent, he is able to finish in just an hour and a half. Michael doesn't try to cram more work into this newly discovered free time. He has accomplished what he had hoped for the day.

Thursday—One Day Before the Exam

Michael feels good. Yes, the exam is tomorrow. But he has already applied the quiz-and-recall method to three-fourths of the material that he needs to learn. While many of his classmates have set aside this entire day (and probably night as well) for cramming, Michael, on the other hand, once again schedules only a couple of hours in the morning.

It takes him a little over an hour to complete his final mega-problem set (this material was covered just last week in class, so it's still fresh in his mind), and with the remaining time he goes through his notes to retrieve the handful of question-marked topics that evaded his efforts, as spelled out in Step #5, to explain them before the study process began. For each of these questions, Michael reduces his confusion to a set of concise statements along the lines of: *"I don't understand the fourth step in the following problem from the 9/28/05 lecture notes..."* He then e-mails a friend in the class (someone who happens to have more natural math ability than Michael), asking if he can stop by to talk about the material. The friend agrees.

That night, Michael stops by his friend's dorm room. Not surprisingly, the friend is bleary eyed, surrounded by piles of notes, and just finishing the first several hours of what will undoubtedly become a late-night cram session. They discuss Michael's specific questions and clear up most of his confusion. The friend makes some comments about how brutal the studying will be, and Michael nods in agreement—choosing not, for the sake of their friendship, to mention that he hasn't even so much as looked at a calculus textbook since early that morning and has no intention of looking at one for the rest of the evening.

Friday—Day of the Exam

If a practice exam had been available, this morning would be a great time for Michael to tackle it. Refreshed and prepared, Michael would have found the experience a confidence booster and a final check for any techniques he might have missed in his systematic review.

Because no such practice exam exists, Michael creates his own. Setting aside forty-five minutes in the morning for a final review,

Michael articulates out loud the explanations that he learned last night for his question-marked topics. He then goes back over a handful of the hardest problems from his mega-problem sets, solving each one with ease. This boosts his confidence and puts his mind in the right state. That's it. He's ready to go.

When the big moment arrives, and the exams are finally handed out, Michael knows exactly how to proceed. He first sorts the questions in order of difficulty and then constructs a time budget. He gets off to a good start, providing solid answers to the easy problems that he tackles first. Soon he is left with only a small number of tricky problems and a solid block of time in which to solve them. He begins work on the first of these hard prompts but quickly finds himself stuck. He's having trouble finding a solution. Time marches forward. Incipient tinges of panic begin to nibble at his concentration.

Michael realizes it's time to step back. He takes a deep breath. Remembering the test-taking strategies from Step #6, he skips this problem and moves on to the next. He is able to get decent answers for the remaining hard problems. They aren't great answers, but they demonstrate his solid understanding of the underlying techniques. Now, with only five minutes to spare, Michael returns to his nemesis. It's still tricky. He still doesn't know exactly how to solve it. But the pressure is much lower now. Because it's the *only* problem left, Michael can rid his mind of the distraction of other questions. This is all that remains; even if he completely blanks and puts down nothing, the only damage done will be limited to one problem. That's not so bad.

With the intensity of the situation lessened, Michael can think more clearly. And, sure enough, he comes up with an idea of how to proceed. In the few minutes that remain, he carefully records some sensible steps toward a solution. It's by no means a complete or perfect response, but it's the best he can do under the circumstances.

The Aftermath

As is often the case, the problem that gave Michael so much trouble gave everyone else in the class trouble as well. Many of these other students, however, didn't have the resources to stay cool under pressure (the resources, of course, being Michael's test-taking strategies). Their consternation regarding this one devilish prompt led them to waste a lot of time, rush through the final problems, and make many careless mistakes. Michael, on the other hand, got credit for all of the problems that he knew and a good chunk of partial credit for the tricky problem. Because of the trouble his classmates had on this exam, his performance, though not perfect, was near the top of the heap. He receives an A.

The lesson learned here is important. For technical exams, you can never guess how well you performed until you get your grade back. Problems that you couldn't solve may have stymied everyone else as well. Therefore, you need to lose the high school mentality that 90 percent to 100 percent of the points gets an A, and 80 percent to 89 percent of the points gets a B, and so forth. In technical classes, it's most likely that the professor grades on a curve, so that the top 15 percent of scores (no matter how high or low they are) get As, the next 20 percent get Bs, and so on. For example, I've taken more than one technical exam where the average score was hovering around 50 points out of 100, and a score of 65 merited an A. I've seen exam questions that not a single person in the class got right. And I once got an A on an exam where I left a problem blank that was worth 25 percent of the points. You never know what's going to happen.

This all leads to the following point: *Never lose your cool.* Michael did the right thing by ordering his problems according to their difficulty and then skipping past a particularly troubling one when it appeared. His goal was to get the maximum number of points possible, not to get every problem right. And the result was a strong grade.

Part Two Cheat Sheet

Step #1. Take Smart Notes

- Always go to class and try to take the best notes possible.

- For nontechnical courses, capture the big ideas by taking notes in the question/evidence/conclusion format.

- For technical courses, record as many sample problems and answers as possible.

Step #2. Demote Your Assignments

- Work a little bit each day on your assignments; avoid suffering from *day-before syndrome*.

- Read only the favored sources on the syllabus in detail. To decide how much time to spend on supplemental sources, remember the importance hierarchy:

  - readings that **make an argument** are more important than

  - readings that **describe an event or person,** which are more important than

  - readings that only **provide context** (i.e., speech transcripts, press clippings).

- Take reading notes in the question/evidence/conclusion format.

- Work in groups on problem sets, solve problems on the go, and write up your answers formally the first time.

Step #3. Marshal Your Resources

- Figure out exactly what the test will cover.

- Cluster your notes for nontechnical courses.

- Build mega-problem sets for technical courses.

Step #4. Conquer the Material

- Embrace the quiz-and-recall method. It's the single most efficient way to study.

- Spread out memorization over several days. Your mind can do only so much at a time.

Step #5. Invest in "Academic Disaster Insurance"

- Eliminate the question marks for topics covered in class or from the reading that you don't understand.

Step #6. Provide "A+" Answers

- Look over the whole test first.

- Figure out how much time you have to spend on each question (leaving a ten-minute cushion at the end).

- Answer the questions in order of increasing difficulty.

- Write out a mini-outline before tackling an essay question.

- Use any and all leftover time to check and recheck your work.

Part 3
Essays and Papers

"I don't believe in sitting in front of
a blank screen and just starting to
write, hoping it will come to you."

Anna, *a straight-A college student*

Paper writing is hard, and, to some extent, this is unavoidable. A college-level paper requires you to sift through endless sources of information, identify insights, form arguments, and then translate the results of these efforts into clean, eloquent prose. In short, a good paper requires a good amount of serious thinking, and that takes time.

Furthermore, this thinking can't all be reduced to a simple system. In high school, you probably had a nice neat format that all papers could fit into—an introduction, which stated a thesis, followed by isolated supporting paragraphs, each providing one piece of evidence, and then finally a conclusion that reiterated the thesis. Those were the days! Unfortunately, this oversimplified system won't work in college. The thinking required for a college-level paper is much more complex. A format that works for an Anthropology essay, for example, might be completely different from a format that works for a History research paper. A piece-by-piece presentation of evidence might be appropriate for one class, but multiple intertwined narratives might be better for another. Each assignment is a fresh challenge, and each demands a lot of attention and care.

However, there is hope. Paper writing is hard, but the good news is that it doesn't have to be as hard as most students make it. Let's begin by taking a closer look at the paper-writing process itself, which can be broken down into three separate components:

1. Sifting through existing arguments.

2. Forming your own argument.

3. Communicating your argument clearly.

Most students approach paper writing by combining all three of these components into one drawn-out and bloated process. They sit down at their computer, stack up some sources, and then begin writing with only a vague idea of where they're headed. Whenever their argument stalls, they flip through their sources until they find an interesting quote, they insert this quote into their document, and then let their argument continue in this new direction for a while, until it stalls once again—at which point, it's back to the sources. This cycle of research/think/write continues slowly for hours as the paper is constructed, one painful paragraph at a time. As you can imagine, this process is incredibly draining. Each of the three components described above is mentally taxing, but to do all three *at the same time* is downright exhausting!

The straight-A approach, on the other hand, is to separate these components into distinct challenges, each of which can be handled by a fine-tuned and efficient system. Each of the three components remains difficult, but by separating them and applying systematic strategies to each, no part of the paper writing process comes even close to the agonizing approach employed by most students. As Gretchen, a straight-A student from Skidmore, emphasizes: "The key to effective paper writing is breaking down the task into manageable units."

The straight-A strategy is made up of eight steps. We start by discussing how to find a topic that will hold your interest and how to locate a thesis within the topic that is both interesting and supportable. From there, we move on to the research effort. This step is crucial, as research, perhaps more than any other part of the paper-writing process, is where the most time can be wasted. We present a streamlined system for gathering and annotating the right material as quickly as possible. After research comes argument construction. There is, unfortunately, no simple system that guarantees a smart argument. But we do describe helpful strategies for gathering feedback on your argument and recording it in an outline format that best facilitates the steps that follow.

Next comes the writing. At this point, you have already figured out exactly what you are going to say and how you are going to support it, so this step has been reduced to constructing clear prose for a well-understood argument. As a result, we don't spend much time here. **The sooner you dispel the notion that writing is the most important part of paper writing, the easier it will become for you to reap the benefits of the straight-A approach.** Anna, a straight-A student from Dartmouth, sums this up succinctly when she notes: "Once I have the structure, the paper writes itself."

Finally, we tackle editing. Some students spend too little time on this step and subsequently hand in papers with stupid grade-busting mistakes. Other students spend way too much time on this step, and thus make the paper-writing process much longer than it need be. To alleviate these problems, we conclude Part Three with a specific three-pass process that will consistently transform your paper into something worthy of submission—without wasted effort.

Don't be intimidated by the number of steps—many of them describe very short (and quite painless) procedures, such as finding a topic or asking your professor for his opinion of your thesis. We separate these small pieces into their own steps, however, because it allows us to focus on their importance and gives you a plan for completing them—even if their time demands are minimal.

One last note: Not all papers are made equal. Writing assignments can vary from a three-page analysis of a book chapter to a fifty-page mini-dissertation based on exhaustive research. In recognition of this variation, we distinguish two different types of writing assignments: *research papers* and *critical analysis essays*. The steps that follow will discuss both of these types separately to ensure that your paper-writing process is as efficient and targeted as possible for each specific assignment.

Research Papers vs. Critical Analysis Essays

Writing assignments come in many varieties. Some require a lot of original research, whereas others require only a critical discussion of a topic introduced in class. Some have ulcer-inducing length requirements, whereas others ask for only a handful of pages. We capture these differences with the simple classification scheme of *research papers* versus *critical analysis essays*. Some assignments, of course, may fall outside of these two descriptions, but, for the most part, they capture the major variations in paper writing. All of the advice that follows explicitly describes which of these two types it applies to.

Research Papers

A research paper requires you to choose a topic within provided parameters and then devise an original thesis relevant to your chosen topic. For example, the broad parameters for your topic choice might be *"anything involving the British Empire,"* the specific topic you choose from within these parameters might be *"public schools and the British Empire,"* and the thesis you choose might be *"the public school system in nineteenth-century England had a curriculum specifically tailored to the requirements of the British Empire."*

Research papers require original research to support your original thesis, and, accordingly, their page lengths are long and their due dates are generally a ways off from when they are assigned. If you spread out the work appropriately and choose the right topic, research papers can provide a rewarding intellectual challenge. Proposing and supporting an original argument is exciting. However, if left until the last minute, these assignments can become a nightmare. More than a few students have suffered a nervous breakdown from the stress of tackling a major research paper at the last moment. So for these assignments in particular, take careful note of the scheduling recommendations that follow.

Critical Analysis Essays

Critical analysis essays are the bread and butter of most liberal arts classes. These essays are short, and they typically require you to analyze one or more of your class reading assignments. They are often set up as a comparison, for example: *"How do Nordlinger and Hopkins differ in their approach to understanding American Isolationism. What cultural and theological sources account for these differences?"*

Critical analysis essays differ from research papers in several significant ways: Topics are provided in advance, your thesis is nothing more than a specific answer to the question asked in the assignment, and there is little-to-no original research required. Not surprisingly, these essays require less time to complete than research papers. Their goal is to test your understanding of the material presented in class, not to seek out and present new ideas.

Don't get the wrong idea—these essays are not necessarily *easier* than research papers. College writing assignments follow a simple rule: **The required precision of your thinking works in direct proportion to the constraint of the material.** That is, the more specific the assignment, the more subtle and detailed your thinking must be. So beware. If your assignment covers only one chapter, then you're going to need to understand every word of that chapter and be able to articulate your analysis with precision.

Step 1

Target a Titillating Topic

Remember: A topic does not equal a thesis. A topic describes an interesting subject or area of observation. A thesis presents an interesting, specific argument *about* that subject or observation. Let's look at some examples:*

Topic	Thesis
There are interesting similarities between the art of Caspar David Friedrich and Washington Allston, even though they	These similarities derive from Friedrich and Allston's shared connection to Samuel Taylor Coleridge and his prescient

*Reader beware: These thesis statements are the product of the author's imagination and are therefore, more likely than not, completely bogus. Use them at your own risk.

worked on different continents. (*observation*)	brand of early postmodern philosophy.
The early work of Faulkner (*subject*)	Faulkner's early style was influenced by the European modernists.
During the first half of the twentieth century, New York's Chinatown boomed while other immigrant communities struggled to find a financial foothold. (*observation*)	The cultural institutions of mainland China, when exported to American immigrant populations, provided a support system and organizational structure well suited to mitigate the specific challenges of building financial security in a new country.

As mentioned, for a critical analysis essay, the topic is provided, so this step won't be applicable. For a research paper, however, you get to choose the topic—so we'll focus on the specific case of research paper topic selection for the remainder of this section.

Choosing a Research Paper Topic

Typically, the professor will provide some loose parameters. For an art history course, these might be: "Any artist covered in the class so far." For a political science class they might be: "Economic policy and Latin America." The key is to choose a topic, within the constraints of the assignment, that excites you. All work that follows on your paper will stem from this topic; if you are not intrigued by the idea, then the paper-writing process will be tedious. If, on the other hand, you are fascinated, or at least curious, then the process will be that much easier.

The best way to identify a titillating topic is to start looking for one early. "I work on topic ideas in my head and on scraps of paper beginning anywhere from a week to a month in advance of the actual deadline for a paper," explains Doris, a straight-A Harvard student. Follow this approach. On the very first day of class, read the description of the research paper(s) that will be assigned. The syllabus should describe each paper's topic parameters, and the professor will usually discuss these assignments briefly early on in the term. Once you know the parameters for the paper, you should constantly be on the lookout for a particular subject or observation that interests you. If one reading assignment really grabs your attention, jot down the topic so you'll remember it later. If a professor poses an interesting question during class, or piques your curiosity by describing a compelling open area of research, make a note of it. As Sean, a straight-A student from Yale, explains: "Keep an eye out for concepts that interest you in the readings and lectures. If there's something that grabs you, it will probably make a good topic."

If you have trouble finding a topic in advance, you have two options. First, as Chien Wen, a straight-A student from Dartmouth, advises: "Approach your professor with some ideas you have and let him recommend some appropriate readings." Professors know their field well, so they should have no trouble pointing you toward some resources to help flesh out your initial thoughts. Second, as Chien Wen also advises: "Read your primary sources carefully." Grab a textbook or similar general source from the class, and then skim through and look for angles that catch your attention, passages that make you ask "why," or descriptions of competing arguments debating an interesting subject. "Be imaginative and intuitive—look for unusual connections between individuals, ideas, and broader themes," says Chien Wen.

In general, the more care you take during this first step, the easier the rest of the paper-writing process will be, so take your topic choice seriously.

Step 2

Conduct a Thesis-Hunting Expedition

Now that you've found a topic that excites you, you need to construct a thesis that makes a compelling argument concerning this topic. Once again, for a critical analysis essay, most of the work toward constructing your thesis has already been done for you. Typically, the essay prompt will contain a specific question (i.e., *"How do the two arguments differ?"* or *"Why does the author say this?"*), and your thesis is a summary of your answer. For a research paper, on the other hand, you might be dealing with a very broad topic that requires significant digging to find an interesting and supportable idea that can be expanded to fit the required page limit.

In both cases, some initial research is required. A thesis devised from scratch is dangerous. Without some initial exploration, you have no idea whether or not your idea is viable, and there are few experiences worse than being forced to restart a paper after many hours of work. At the same time, however, you don't want to dedicate days to intensively reading every book in the field in search of a perfect thesis, because this would be inefficient.

For a critical analysis essay, the solution is simple: Review both the reading notes and lecture notes that relate to the essay prompt. And that's it! This should provide a rough idea of how you are going to answer the question posed by the assignment. Therefore, your thesis has been found. Even though it's simple, don't skip this step for critical analysis essays. The earlier you develop an idea of what you are going to say, the more time you have to refine the nuances of your argument.

For research papers, on the other hand, the task of finding a thesis is more complicated. No sources have been preselected for you, and no specific question has been provided. All you have is a general topic that you thought up yourself. Now you must wade into a vast sea of knowledge and somehow find enough material to devise a strong thesis—while avoiding drowning in the sheer volume of available information.

Not surprisingly, the straight-A students interviewed for this book have mastered the art of conducting research paper thesis-hunting expeditions. Their goals are twofold: (1) find an interesting thesis that can be supported within the scope of the assignment; and (2) minimize the time required to conduct this search. Accomplishing both of these goals sounds hard, but straight-A students get it done. What's their secret? One simple phrase: *Start general, then move one layer deep.* Let's take a closer look at what this really means.

Start General, Then Move One Layer Deep

"I usually begin with basic sources," explains Chris, a straight-A student from Dartmouth. "If I'm doing a paper on the Kurds in Turkey, for example, I get a recently published general history on this topic." Similarly, if your topic is Faulkner's early writing, you might find one or two Faulkner biographies and then focus only on the chapters dealing with his early years. If you have a hard time finding a few general sources for your topic, then ask your professor—he'll have plenty of titles to recommend. In addition, keep in mind that most courses set up a reserve shelf at the campus library. This shelf contains books that were selected by the professor because of their relevance to the course. Typically, you can check out reserve books for only a couple of hours at a time, so they should always be available to the students who need them. This is a great place to find general sources.

So that's step one (the "start general" part of the strategy). The reason we need a second step is because you shouldn't expect to find your thesis idea in a general source. Of course, you *might* get lucky and find an interesting thesis during this first step. In general, however, overview sources will be much too broad to reveal a targeted and interesting argument that hasn't already been written about extensively.

The main reason you found these general sources is to get at their bibliographies. As Chris goes on to explain: "I read any chapters from my general sources that look useful for my paper. I then look up the sources used in that chapter." In other words, the second step of your thesis-hunting expedition is to examine the list of books and articles cited in the relevant sections of your general sources. From this list, choose the cited works that look the most promising, and then go find them in the library. These sources will be more focused—perhaps journal articles or books addressing only a small number of specific arguments. You are most likely to come across an interesting and appropriately targeted thesis idea using these more focused sources.

Let's apply this approach to our Faulkner example from before. Perhaps one of our general sources cites a journal article on the influence of a specific European modernist writer on Faulkner. You find this journal article, and while reviewing it you notice that it mentions, in passing, a list of other modernist writers who might have had a similar influence. *Aha!* Now this could be an interesting thesis. You might choose one of these modernists from the list and then look for historical evidence of their connection to the primary writer.

Perhaps, instead, one of the general sources talks about a period of Faulkner's life that he spent in Europe. Maybe it also mentions that our only records of this travel are letters written by the young author himself, and then it provides a citation to a collection of these letters. You then locate these letters, begin to read through them, and notice that he mentions a particular bar in London several times. This too might be a source of a fascinating thesis. You could investigate the intellectual climate of London nightspots of the time and posit their potential influence on Faulkner's work. From there, perhaps the core of your paper could be to present a piece of writing from right before the trip, and another from right after, and then argue which stylistic changes may have been influenced by his foray into the intellectual intensity of the London literary milieu. The key is to keep in mind that even very small observations can lead to large, interesting discussions.

How do you know your thesis idea is good enough to support an insightful paper? "A great thesis typically has at least these four qualities," explains Christine, a straight-A student from Harvard. "It's provocative, nuanced, direct, and inclusive." She goes on to warn: "A thesis should, at the same time, also show a grasp of the complexities of a subject—'in this poem, X symbolizes Y because Z' is a weak type of thesis structure, far too reductive and simplistic—don't be afraid to leave room for ambiguity and unresolved issues." Wendy, a straight-A student from Amherst, puts it simply: "The most important part of your paper is the thesis. Once you have a solid thesis, the rest just falls into place."

Here's the tricky part: Your thesis will change and evolve as you continue the paper-writing process. This is inevitable, because you haven't done your exhaustive research yet. At this early stage, your thesis more likely explains the *type* of connection or answer you hope to find, rather than the final connections and answers themselves. To revisit our Faulkner example, your early research may indicate that the social milieu of a certain London nightspot influenced a young Faulkner, but you might not yet know all the ways this influence was manifest. More research is required, and that's okay. You should embrace this evolution of your ideas as the process continues. For now, it's sufficient that your fledgling thesis looks like it's on the path toward fulfilling the properties mentioned above. In other words, before continuing, make sure that your preliminary research strongly indicates that something similar to your thesis idea will be supported by the more detailed investigations to follow. Be honest with yourself: If you made up your thesis simply because it sounded cool, but have no real reason to believe it to be true, then you're courting a paper-writing disaster. If, on the other hand, several pieces of early evidence point to the types of interesting connections described by your thesis, then you're on the right track.

Step 3

Seek a
Second Opinion

At this point you should have an interesting topic and a targeted thesis. You're well on your way toward a standout paper, but don't get too far ahead of yourself. It's time to take a step back.

More than a few students have dived deep into the paper-writing process, supported by what they thought was a compelling thesis, only to find out many pages later that their premise was not as strong as it initially seemed. Perhaps they fail to find enough evidence to support the argument. Perhaps they stumble across another source that has already made the exact same point. Or, as is often the case, perhaps they find their thesis to be too broad to be succinctly argued within the scope of a paper assignment.

The thesis-hunting tips of the last step help eliminate this possibility, but they're not enough by themselves. Once you think you have a good thesis, a final step remains before diving fully into the research and writing process. As Rielle, a straight-A student from Brown, explains: "I often talk to a professor to clarify my ideas before I begin writing." This is great advice. For every research paper and significant critical analysis essay (i.e., assignments more than just a few pages long), you should make a habit of discussing your targeted thesis idea with your professor. Go to office hours, or make an appointment, explain your topic and thesis, then ask the following questions:

1. Is my idea appropriate for the assignment?

2. Does it cover too much?

3. Is it too simple?

For a critical analysis essay, if the professor deems your thesis appropriate, this is a good sign that you are not going to get stuck. You can now move ahead with confidence. For a research paper, if the professor deems your thesis appropriate, take advantage of this time to explain some of the sources you plan to examine. The professor will likely have some additional sources to suggest. Write these down. This just saved you some serious research time! For both types of papers, if the professor isn't enthusiastic about your thesis idea, then he or she will likely help you adjust it into something that is reasonable.

When you leave this meeting, which should require only ten to twenty minutes, you will have confidence in the foundation of your paper. You can now move full speed into the research stage without fear of reaching a devastating dead end later on in the process. It's amazing how many students ignore this incredible resource. One simple meeting can make the difference between a standout work and an incoherent dud.

Remember, this step is not intended as a shortcut. If you skipped the previous step and show up at office hours without a targeted idea, the professor is not going to give you one for free. However, as Christine from Harvard explains: "They'll rarely refuse to listen if they see you've thought things out in advance."

Step 4

Research like a Machine

Not surprisingly, research is the domain of the research paper. For a critical analysis essay, your sources are already specified, and there are probably only one or two of them. Therefore, when working on an essay, you can skip this step and move on to Step #5 (Craft a Powerful Story), which describes how to organize your argument.

For research papers, however, the following advice is crucial. Why? Because how you research can make or break your paper-writing efforts. If your strategy is haphazard—as is the case with most students—then two immediate problems will arise. First, the writing process will become frustrating and tedious, since you will be forced to continually stop and seek out new sources to extend your argument. Second, and more important, the resulting paper will be weak. A good argument requires a solid grasp of all relevant information.

You want all the necessary facts and ideas to be at your fingertips, easily manipulated, sourced, and shuffled, as you build your case. If your sources are incomplete and disorganized, then your paper will be, too.

On the other hand, you can also run the risk of spending too much time on research. Many eager students have succumbed to the horrors of *research recursion syndrome*—an unhealthy need to go find "just one more source," often leading to hours and hours of wasted time, dorm rooms overwhelmed with teetering stacks of books, and one seriously sleep-deprived student. This is grind territory, and you should avoid it at all costs. So while at first glance it may seem easier than choosing a thesis or writing the paper itself, in fact the research step of paper writing is easy to get wrong.

Fortunately, straight-A students have figured out a way to walk the research tightrope—getting the information they need without becoming lost amid the endless available sources. Their strategy can be summarized by a simple phrase: **Research like a machine**. They follow a system—a mechanical process, the same for every paper—that produces consistent high-quality results. Feed them a thesis, watch their wheels turn, and then out pops a set of photocopied, organized, and annotated notes. Their system ensures that the quality of their research is sufficient to fuel a standout paper and at the same time requires the minimum amount of time to achieve this goal.

Sounds pretty cool, right? But how does it work? Their system is based on these four steps:

1. Find sources.

2. Make personal copies of all sources.

3. Annotate the material.

4. Decide if you're done. (If the answer is "no," then loop back to #1.)

That's it. The devil, of course, is in the details. So let's take a closer look at what each of the steps entails.

1. Find Sources

There are two types of sources: general and specific. As described in Step #2, the former include overviews of your topic (i.e., biography or textbook), whereas the latter focus on specific arguments (i.e., a journal article or book about a specific event or idea). For a college-level paper, most of your best information is going to come from specific sources. The hard part, of course, is finding them.

There are two strategies that can help you accomplish this goal. The first is stolen straight from Step #2: Start with general sources and then look in their bibliographies for more targeted resources. As David, a straight-A student from Dartmouth, says: "Once you have two or three materials that you like, it's all about the bibliographies . . . find out where the author found the fuel for his arguments and go check those out." In Step #2, I suggested that you ask your professor or browse the course reserve shelf to find some of these general sources. Another place to look is your library's online card catalog. This sounds obvious, but using an online catalog correctly is not a trivial task. Just typing in keywords might not turn up every book that deals with your topic of interest. You need some more advanced tricks.

One such trick is to take advantage of the Library of Congress

(LOC) topic classifications. What are these? The Library of Congress tries to classify all books into one large hierarchy of topics. For example, Heinrich Harrer's fascinating book *The White Spider* (an account of the first team to ascend the infamous North Face of the Eiger Mountain) is described by the following two classifications:

1. Mountaineering—Switzerland—Eiger—History

2. Eiger (Switzerland)—Description and travel

When you find a book in an online card catalog, its corresponding LOC topic classifications should be listed. The cool part is that these topics should also be hyperlinked. That is, if you found an entry for *The White Spider*, you could click on Mountaineering—Switzerland—Eiger—History to return a list of *every* book in the library under this classification. Therefore, if you find one general source on a topic, then you can easily find many others. And once you have found general sources, you can turn to their bibliographies to find something more specific.

The second strategy for finding specific sources is to search for them directly. This approach is important. Not every specific source relevant to your thesis can be found in the bibliography of a general source. This is particularly true for more recent scholarship. Books take a long time to write; if a paper was published only within the last few years, it is probably too soon to find a general tome that cites it.

The problem here is that specific sources can be difficult to find. For example, continuing with the Eiger topic introduced above, let's say your thesis within this topic is: "The many failed attempts to ascend the North Face of the Eiger played an important role in the development of Swiss cultural identity during the first half of the twentieth century." Finding a *general source* about the Eiger, such as *The White Spider*, is easy enough. But finding a targeted source on the impact of the Eiger on Swiss cultural identity will be significantly more complicated. Simply typing "the impact of the Eiger on Swiss cultural identity" into the library card catalog probably won't turn up many hits. So how do you locate these elusive specific sources? There are four main search tactics.

Search Tactic #1: Break Up Your Query into General Chunks

If you can reduce your specific query to a group of related, yet succinct, general searches, you will have a much better chance of finding a relevant source. Following the Eiger example, you might try:

- Alpine hiking Switzerland culture

- Switzerland cultural identity

- Alpine hiking

- Mountaineering Switzerland

Any one of these more general queries could turn up a source that either directly references your thesis or makes a point that supports your thesis. With practice, you will get better at constructing these general probes aimed at illuminating a specific idea.

Search Tactic #2: Use Journal Databases

As mentioned, specific sources are more likely to be scholarly articles than books. Your library card catalog does not index articles.

Therefore, as Chris from Dartmouth recommends, you should consider "article database searches (like JSTOR) on the specific topic."

How do you find these databases? Your library Web site should contain a list of available electronic resources. At some point during your freshman year, you will probably be given an orientation on this topic. (Even if you sleep through it, as most of us do, it shouldn't be that hard to figure out.) This list of resources is usually broken up by academic concentration (i.e., Political Science, Anthropology, and so forth). Go to the concentration relevant to your paper, and you should see a list of searchable archives. Many of these resources will be databases of scholarly articles, so search these focused databases using the general search term chunks described in the preceding tactic and see what pops up.

If your topic is interdisciplinary, meaning that it draws from multiple academic concentrations, follow Chris's advice and try a big database like JSTOR (http://www.jstor.org), which contains scholarly articles on a large variety of academic topics.

Search Tactic #3: When in Doubt, Google

"Google is your friend, first and foremost," says David from Dartmouth. This is good advice—as Google is a great tool—but it should be used with some caution. A good rule of thumb is: **Don't cite Web sites**. Academics don't trust them. Journal articles go through extensive peer-reviewing before they are published, and academic books are written by experts and rigorously edited. On Web sites, however, anything goes. Therefore, they're worthless in terms of supporting an argument. Referencing Web sites is something you do in high school.

If you do this in college, be prepared to experience the wrath of your professor.

This being said, Google is still immensely useful. Not for finding Web sites to cite, but for finding Web sites that reference books and articles relevant to your thesis. For example, a search for "Eiger and Swiss Cultural Identity" might actually turn up some Web sites dealing with, or related to, this obscure issue. The Google search algorithm is a lot smarter than the one used by card catalogs, so even very complicated queries can turn up surprisingly accurate results. If you're lucky, some of these Web sites will mention specific sources— a book name or article title. Now you can look up *these* in your card catalog, and then treat them like any other formal source.

Search Tactic #4: Ask a Librarian

Most college libraries are staffed with reference librarians who want nothing more than to help you find the information that you seek. It's what they're paid to do, and they're great at it. Too many students, however, ignore this wonderful resource. Here you have experts who can save you hours of struggle by conducting advanced searches on your behalf; yet most students never think to take advantage of the opportunity.

Making a visit to the reference desk should be one of your first steps when researching a challenging assignment. Simply explain your topic and thesis to the librarian, and he or she will walk you through several searches. Not only will this identify some specific sources that you may have otherwise missed, but it will also expose you to new library resources and databases that you can now use for future projects. The more time you spend with reference librarians, the better you will become at finding solid material on your own.

2. Make Personal Copies of All Sources

How you handle the sources makes a big difference in the overall efficiency of the paper-writing process. Though there are many ways to deal with the book chapters and articles relevant to your research efforts, many of the straight-A students interviewed for this book favored the following strategy: **Make a photocopy or printout of all relevant material.** If you find a book that has two chapters related to your topic, photocopy those two chapters. If you find an important journal article, photocopy the entire article. If you find an article online, or a relevant Web site, print it out. The goal is to create your own personal hard copy of all sources.

The advantages of this approach are numerous. First, these hard copies are portable. It's easier to carry around a stack of photocopies than a stack of books and journals, so you can take your research with you to your secret study spots or office hours. Second, the information is more accessible. No flipping through big tomes or searching your computer hard drive; all the relevant information is stored in one condensed stack. You can now physically organize your sources, for example, by putting them into piles by author, clustering relevant arguments together with paper clips, or dividing them into folders labeled by subject. As Sean, a straight-A student from Yale, explains: "It's often easier to grasp something when you have a hard copy in front of you." Third, you can mark them up with impunity. "Printouts and Xeroxes of source info are often superior to books or digital copies," explains Christine from Harvard, "since you can annotate them to death." Feel free to underline things, highlight, draw arrows, cross out sections, or put big stars next to important points.

In general, this approach maximizes the control you have over your information, ensuring that your sources work for you. However, there are a couple of important caveats to remember. First, make sure you label each photocopy with all of the information needed to later construct a formal citation. For example, if you photocopy a book chapter, jot down on the first page the name of the book, the author(s), the publisher and its location, and the copyright date. Or, if you prefer, follow Christine's advice and simply "make a photocopy of the title and copyright info" as found in the front of the book, so you can use it later while constructing the works cited for your paper and ensure that you don't find yourself "running back to the library at the last moment for citation info."

Second, photocopy each source's bibliography. This way, if you come across an interesting reference in one of your photocopies, you will have easy access to the full citation attached to the reference. For articles, the bibliography is almost always listed immediately following the article. For books using the endnote format, you might have to flip to the back to find the bibliography for a specific chapter.

3. Annotate the Material

Finding a source, of course, is just the first step. A stack of photocopied pages is worthless if you don't know what information it contains and how it might be useful to your paper. You need to review the sources and annotate them with a concise description of the important information, if any, that they contain.

Be careful how you proceed here. Your first instinct might be to follow the advice described in Part Two about how to take notes on your reading assignments. Don't do this—it's overkill. For now, you should be content to follow the advice of David from Dartmouth, who recommends that you "skim, skim, skim." Specifically, read through the source quickly. Every time you pass by an important definition, idea, or opinion that seems relevant to your thesis, jot down (on your computer or by hand) the page number and a *quick* description. For example, if the author argues a particular point of interest, write only what this point is—there is no need to also copy down the evidence he uses to support it as you would for notes on a reading assignment. If the source is a book, then, as Anna from Dartmouth explains: "Pick out only the chapters that relate to the specific aspect of the topic that you are interested in . . . it is not necessary to read the entire book!" When you're finished, staple your annotations to your personal copy of the corresponding source.

In general, proper source annotations should act as concise pointers, containing just enough information to show you where the relevant arguments are hiding. In the next step, where you organize all of your gathered information into a coherent structure, these simple annotations turn out to be exactly what you need to quickly assess the importance of each source. Therefore, you will end up needing to carefully read *only* the passages that help your paper. You should not think of this step as adding work. As you will soon discover, these concise annotations are actually going to save you a significant amount of time.

4. Decide If You're Done

There is no simple answer to this question. While it would be nice to offer a perfect formula for how much research is enough, it is impossible—there are just too many variations to contend with. Some short papers might require dozens of sources, while some long tracts may focus entirely on a handful of original documents.

What follows is a *rough* procedure that should aid your decision about whether or not you have gathered enough research. Remember, this is just an approximation. Always keep in mind the context of your specific assignment. However, this approach should help reduce the guesswork involved in completing this step.

The Research Termination Determination Procedure:

1. List the topics (specific questions, facts, or accounts from your research) that are *crucial* to support your thesis.

2. List the topics that *might* help you support your thesis.

3. If you have at least two good sources for each of the topics from #1, and have at least one good source for a majority of the topics from #2, then you're done. Otherwise, you need to keep researching.

The reason these criteria are just an approximation is because at this early stage you probably don't know exactly how your thesis argument will proceed, so you don't know exactly what information you need. This procedure simply helps you estimate as best you can. By separating out the crucial from the potentially helpful, you are less likely to get stuck hunting down an obscure piece of information that you could do without. This approach is advised by David from Dartmouth, who describes the following similar procedure for sorting his research sources: "I make three piles of my sources: very useful, potentially useful, and not useful." To draw from our previous example, if your thesis deals with the Eiger and Swiss cultural identity, you might construct your list of "crucial" and "might help" topics as follows:

1. **Topics that are crucial to support the thesis:**
   - Basic historical information concerning the Eiger (when it was discovered, when it was first climbed, and so forth)

   - Arguments concerning Swiss cultural identity at the turn of the century

2. **Topics that might be helpful in supporting the thesis:**
   - Memoirs of people who were involved in the first ascents of the mountain

   - Press accounts from the time (both Swiss and non-Swiss)

   - General discussions of the role of sports and national pride

If you have a hard time tracking down one of the topics from the second list, you would still be okay. If, on the other hand, you have a hard time tracking down either of the topics from the first list, then you need to keep looking.

In the next step, where you actually begin to outline your paper, it's expected that you might need to return briefly to the research phase and find additional sources to fill in any holes. If you follow the procedure above, however, you will minimize the amount of secondary research that you are forced to conduct—thus saving yourself from more hours in the library.

Step 5

Craft a Powerful Story

This step is where the magic happens. It's the fun part of paper writing—the moment of intellectual eureka. You have already defined (and verified) a compelling thesis, and you have at your disposal a collection of well-organized and annotated research material. Now it's time to stretch your mental muscles and pull these pieces together into a powerful story. As Anna from Dartmouth says: "In order to write a great paper, you really need to make connections that other people haven't made, and the only way to do that is to think." This is the step where such thinking occurs.

Formulate Your Argument

"You *must* have a vision of what the overall structure of your paper will be," explains Frank, a straight-A student from Brown. "Organization of thought can make a decently researched essay into a fine piece of academic work." Formulating a solid argument, however, cannot be reduced to a system; it is a mental exercise that requires critical thinking and creativity. At the college level, there is no set structure that allows you to fill in the blanks and automatically produce a smart paper. As mentioned in the opening to Part Three, the intro/body/conclusion nonsense introduced in high school won't do you any good here. It's too simplistic, and your professors will be expecting more.

In general, a good college-level argument should accomplish the following:

1. Draw from previous work on the same topic to define the context for the discussion.

2. Introduce a thesis and carefully spell out how it relates to existing work on similar issues.

3. Support the thesis with careful reasoning and references to existing arguments, evidence, and primary sources.

4. Introduce some final prognostications about extending the argument and its potential impact on the field as a whole.

There is, however, no set order or format for presenting these general points. One paper might start by defining the context and then move on to the thesis. Another paper might start with the thesis, argue it, and then introduce the broader context at the end. Many papers might interweave all four points. There is no right answer here. And the hard truth is that the only way to get better at organizing and presenting your thoughts is through practice. So write a lot and read good arguments a lot. This is the best recipe for developing your skills for this step.

That being said, there are some *general* pointers about how to go about formulating your argument. These aren't rules for what to say; rather, they are tips for how to get your brain fired up and your creative juices flowing.

Tip #1: When it comes time to craft the storyline of your paper, put yourself in the right mind-set. Grab a copy of *Atlantic Monthly, The New Yorker, Harper's*, or any other publication that features well-crafted discussions. Peruse some articles, and then go for a walk along a quiet path. Alternatively, as David from Dartmouth recommends: "Talk to friends—if they are good friends they will allow you to bounce ideas off of them and talk through your work." You can also cloister yourself in a dusty, wooden-shelved, overstuffed-armchair-filled corner of the library, or argue with your professor during office hours. Reread related articles and chapters from your course syllabus. Watch a PBS documentary. Do whatever it takes to get the reasoning portions of your mind inspired and curious.

Tip #2: At this point, grab your source material from the previous step. If your assignment is a critical analysis essay, this will consist of only a couple of books and your reading notes. If it's a research paper, you might have a large stack of photocopied chapters and articles. In either case, dive into this information, and start letting the relevant facts and arguments settle into your mind. This is where your annotations will point you toward what's interesting, and help you avoid the irrelevant.

Tip #3: Take a break. Do something else. Let the pieces float around in the background noise of your mind. "The first thing I do when I have a paper to write is take a nap," explains Laura, a straight-A student from Dartmouth. "I crawl into bed and just think . . . as long as I'm thinking about the subject when I fall asleep, I will dream about the material and usually come up with some sort of interesting idea." Similarly, start looking for any opportunity to do a little thinking about your argument. "I think about my paper when I go around completing my daily chores, when I walk to class or when I wait on line in the dining hall," explains Anna from Dartmouth. Use this downtime to slide the pieces of your argument around in your head and play with the structure a bit. Keep returning to your research material as needed to find more details and to increase your understanding. You need to expose yourself to the source material again and again to fully internalize it. Only then can you really pull together the best possible argument.

Constructing an Outline

You need an outline to capture the argument you just spent so much time devising. Keep in mind, however, that all outlines are *not* created equal. In fact, there are two major outline-related mistakes made by students. First: *under-outlining*. If your outline lacks enough detail, it's not going to serve its purpose as a structure to guide your writing, and you will end up writing from scratch. You want to avoid this at all costs; it leads to argumentative dead ends and weak structure overall. "In high school, I wrote all my papers in one go, starting with the intro, constructing and polishing each sentence in order," explains Christine from Harvard. "In college I've become a huge fan of outline-based writing, which has made my essays much more tightly argued and given them better, clearer trajectories ... since I can now shuffle topics around until they flow with some natural order and logic—rather than straining rhetorically to bridge from one idea to another."

The second mistake: *over-outlining*. Some students construct beautifully intricate outlines, replete with three or four levels of information, roman numerals, digits, letters, and tabs flying everywhere—the type of outline they taught you to make for your fifth-grade research project. Don't do this either. It constrains you. As Doris from Harvard explains: "One pitfall to avoid is getting stuck in the outline stage—I've seen students who spend far too much time embellishing their outlines when they should really have begun writing the paper itself long ago." When it comes time to write, you will be hampered if you constructed an outline that practically spells out what each sentence of each paragraph should say. These sorts of low-level decisions should be made when you write, not before. It's not until you're actually putting words on paper that you will understand the best way to make each small piece of your argument flow. Don't let an outline make these decisions for you.

The happy medium between these two extremes is to construct a topic-level outline. Before we can cover the specifics of this process, I must first define what I mean by "topic." Here, I use the term to describe any self-contained point that you might discuss in your paper. Typically, this is something more general than a piece of evidence but also more specific than a multipart argument. For example, here are some sample topics for our hypothetical paper about the Eiger:

- Our thesis about the Eiger and Swiss cultural identity

- Early written accounts of the Eiger

- The first ascent of the Eiger

- Contemporary press accounts of Eiger summit attempts

- Mentions of the Eiger in early-twentieth-century popular culture

- Mentions of the Eiger in early-twentieth-century Swiss tourist brochures

- MacMillan's thesis about the Alps and European identity

- The relationship between our thesis and MacMillan's argument

- Concluding thoughts about our thesis—implications and future work

We start the outlining process by constructing a topic skeleton. This is a list of all the topics you will discuss in your paper, presented in the order that you plan to include them. Type this list directly into your computer because you will later need the ability to insert text in between items.

Your topic skeleton succinctly describes the structure of your argument. For example, we might take the previously mentioned topics and order them as follows to form a topic skeleton for our hypothetical Eiger paper:

1. Mentions of the Eiger in early-twentieth-century Swiss tourist brochures

2. MacMillan's thesis about the Alps and European identity

3. Our thesis about the Eiger and Swiss cultural identity

4. Early written accounts of the Eiger

5. The first ascent of the Eiger

6. Contemporary press accounts of Eiger summit attempts

7. Mentions of the Eiger in early-twentieth-century popular culture

8. The relationship between our thesis and MacMillan's argument

9. Concluding thoughts about our thesis—implications and future work

At this point, no specific pieces of evidence are described by our outline, but it does capture how the paper will flow. In a perfect world, you would have at least one or two good sources to support each topic. However, it will often occur that as you formulate your topic skeleton, you come across a topic that you really need to include but for which you don't yet have any sources. That's okay. We mentioned at the end of the last step that once you start formulating your argument, you might come across some holes that need to be filled. This is exactly where these holes will become noticeable. Once you have completed your topic skeleton, you need to return to the previous step and find sources to support any of the currently unsupported topics. If you followed the research termination determination procedure from before, there shouldn't be too many of these holes.

Filling in the Details of Your Topic Outline

Once you finish your topic skeleton, and find sources for all of the unsupported topics, it's time to fill in the supporting details. This next step is crucial. As Christine from Harvard explains: "Below each bold header [in my topic skeleton], I compile in regular typeface the evidence pertaining to that header." You should actually type quotes from your research material right into the word processor document containing the outline, and label each quote with the source and page that it came from. For example, under the "first ascent of the Eiger" topic from above, you might insert quotes from a few different books on the mountain as well as excerpts from several contemporary articles. Some of these latter excerpts may also be included under the "contemporary press accounts of Eiger summit attempts" topic. It's okay to share information between topics at this point, since you will sort out which quote to use where once the writing process begins. This is not a time for caution—if it seems relevant, stick it in.

At first, this step may sound excessive. By the time you finish, your outline will be large and filled with quotes, perhaps even longer than the projected length of your completed paper. Fortunately, this process is greatly simplified by the format of your gathered research materials. Because you made a personal copy of and annotated every source, finding the appropriate pieces of evidence to include in your outline will be much easier than if you had to page through each book and article from scratch. Furthermore, the benefits of this outline far outweigh the annoyance of constructing it. As Robert, a straight-A student from Brown, explains; "I find that using this process helps me avoid digging through a pile of books and articles for each piece of information I need as I need it during writing."

Remember, the goal of the straight-A approach is to separate the different components of paper construction. When it comes time to write, you don't want to be flipping through your sources, hunting down the right support. This drains your energy, increases your pain, takes time, and reduces the quality of your writing. This is why it is crucial that you extract the information from your sources in advance. Later, the writing process will be reduced to the much simpler task of simply building a framework around this already identified and organized information structure.

Step 6

Consult Your Expert Panel

"I discuss ideas with friends," says Suzanne, a straight-A student from Brown, "and am therefore usually pretty confident with my argument by the time I sit down to write." Suzanne reinforces a key observation: The more input you receive, the better your paper will turn out. And because soliciting advice is easy, you might as well get your outline reviewed by a group of people you trust. In the straight-A lexicon, this strategy is called "consulting your expert panel." The technique is popular because it requires little effort on your part, but the impact on your paper quality is significant. This is the final push that transforms your thinking from interesting into compelling and your paper from competent into a standout.

Choosing Your Expert Panel

The size of your expert panel should be directly proportional to the importance of the assignment. If it's a one-page essay worth 5 percent of your grade, then your expert panel should consist of only yourself. If it's a medium-size critical analysis essay, you might aim for two opinions. If it's a major term paper worth a significant portion of your grade, than you may want to solicit feedback from as many as half-a-dozen well-chosen people.

Who should sit on your panel? Your number one pick should be your professor. Unless he specifically states that he won't discuss drafts in progress (which professors sometimes do to avoid an overload of conferencing in a large class), definitely plan to bring your outline to office hours. Lay out the general shape of your argument, and the types of sources you are drawing from and where. More often than not, the professor will have some targeted advice on how to better present your points. He might suggest a new order or an added topic that should be addressed. As David from Dartmouth notes, this meeting also "will help you to create a rapport with the prof, and give you an idea of what he or she is looking for."

Yes, you've already talked with your professor in Step #3 (Seek a Second Opinion). Don't worry. There is nothing wrong with talking to a professor on two separate occasions for one paper. The first conference was quick and dealt with making sure you were starting off in the right direction. This second conference is more detailed, making sure that you managed to stay on course. Keep in mind that some students talk to their professors many times during the paper-writing process, perhaps once or twice a week. This is overkill and shouldn't be necessary if you've followed the efficient strategy laid out in this book. But rest assured that two visits are hardly monopolizing your professor's time.

In addition to your professor, as David also suggests, "if you have smart friends, get their help too." Friends from the same class are your best bet, since they will already understand the constraints of the assignment. If you aren't close with any classmates, then tap a friend with a compatible academic background. For example, if your paper is for a history class, it makes more sense to talk to a liberal arts major than an engineering major. The former will be more familiar with this style of paper.

Pick a half-hour period to sit down with each friend you chose. Explain your thesis and then run through your outline, touching on your main supporting arguments. Your friends will help you identify pieces of your structure that are unclear or unnecessary. As Jason, a straight-A student from the University of Pennsylvania, explains: "If you can explain why your argument works in a rational, step-by-step manner, and you have an arsenal of sources to cite to support the argument, then you're ready to go."

One final warning: Before discussing with a classmate, make sure that collaboration of this sort is allowed. It should be no problem for research papers, but for focused critical analysis essays the professor may specifically forbid that you discuss your response with other people from the class.

Step 7

Write Without the Agony

If you've followed the Straight-A strategy so far, writing should be the most straightforward part of constructing a standout paper. This step is not mysterious. At this point, you know what to say and in what order, so all you have to do is clearly communicate your already well-developed argument. "Once I have the outline, my brain relaxes," explains Jeremy, a straight-A student from Dartmouth. "I don't need to think anymore about structuring the paper, but rather just think about how to best articulate my thoughts."

Note, however, that this book is not about the mechanics of writing. This is a skill that you will need to develop on your own. In general, the more you write outside of class, the better; so, to improve your skills, try to write as much as you can. Also, don't be afraid to plunk a *Chicago Manual of Style* above your desk or flip through well-known style guides like William Zinsser's *On Writing Well*. These can help you focus and polish your writing, and professors appreciate clear exposition.

This being said, there is not much left to cover. You know what you have to do: Put words on paper. It's not easy, but, if you followed the previous steps, it won't be nearly as agonizing as most students make it. I leave you with only three succinct pieces of logistical advice to help guide you through the process of combining your writing skills with your straight-A preparation to produce the best possible paper:

Separate Your Writing from the Steps That Come Before and After

As Greta, a straight-A student from Dartmouth, explains, when it comes to the writing process she "would map out a schedule, for example, write two pages a day for five days, and then edit one day." Ryan, another Dartmouth student, admits that he "usually gave about two days for the actual writing, but the research part of the paper usually happened a few weeks before." Both of these students' habits are instructed by a simple rule: Separate your research from your writing and your writing from your editing.

Of course, this is not always practical for a small critical analysis essay, but it's crucial for a more substantial research paper. A fresh mind produces better results. It's hard to write well when you've spent an exhausting morning researching in the library. It's equally as hard to edit carefully when you have already spent hours that day writing the words you are about to review. "Having time away from the paper," explains Jeremy from Dartmouth, "allows you to come at it with better concentration."

Write in Quiet Isolation

Writing requires substantial concentration. If you work in an area with a lot of ambient noise, you will become distracted and your efficiency will decrease dramatically. Therefore, if you have a laptop, retreat to a distant, silent corner of a faraway building to work on your writing. "I am most productive," explains Suzanne from Brown, "in a place where I have total silence and no external stimulation—for example, the library stacks." As I emphasized in Part One of this book, avoid, if possible, study lounges, crowded areas of the library, and public computer labs. These places are noisy, and, as Rielle from Brown warns: "You're always running into people and getting snagged by fascinating conversations." If you don't have a laptop, then work at the computer in your room at times when your roommates are in class or at meetings. If necessary, arrange in advance to kick them out for a few hours so you can work in peace. In addition, you should schedule your writing to correspond to your energetic high points during the day. For me, this meant working right after breakfast with my first cup of coffee. For others, this might be the early evening, right before dinner, or the afternoon after a post-lunch workout. **The key is to recognize that writing is perhaps the most demanding (in terms of focus required) intellectual activity you will do while a college student.** More so than reading, solving problem sets, or studying, writing demands all the energy and focus that you can manage.

Follow Your Outline and Move Slowly

Chris from Dartmouth offers simple advice for tackling the writing process: "I use the outline I've created as a guide and just sort of build from that, taking it one paragraph at a time." Follow this example. Use your outline to direct your writing, setting up and expounding on each of the topics in a clear, cogent way, and copying and pasting quotes directly into your paper wherever needed. Keep your attention focused on the topic at hand. Your mind is free from concerns of structure and sources at this point, so you can concentrate on articulating specific points clearly and strongly.

Always make sure your current point reads clearly before moving on to the next. Some students have success by writing their first draft quickly and sloppily, and then returning to clean it up in many successive editing rounds. In your case, however, because you're working from a detailed topic outline, it will end up being quicker to write carefully the first time. Moving fast tends to produce time-consuming dead ends later on, and ultimately necessitates major rewrites.

And, believe it or not, that's all you need to know. So stop fearing writing! If you follow this system, this step, though still challenging, won't take an excessive amount of time. Leave the all-nighters to the average students, get your first draft done quickly and effectively, and then go have some fun.

Step 8

Fix, Don't Fixate

Editing your paper is important, and this shouldn't come as a surprise. If you hand in pages containing spelling and grammatical mistakes, the professor will be more than disappointed—she's likely to lower your grade as a result. Even if your argument is brilliant, it's really hard to get past those simple errors. This last step of the paper-writing process aims to free your work of these imperfections.

At the same time, however, you don't want to overedit. Many students fixate on these fixes, and end up devoting hours to reviewing draft after draft. This act of academic self-flagellation is especially prevalent when working on big research papers. After all the work you dedicate to crafting a masterpiece of an argument, you begin to fear letting your baby out into the world. It's sort of like suffering from a nerdy version of Stockholm Syndrome—and it's a drag. "You can edit a paper forever and still not be satisfied," explains Frank from Brown. "So it's important to know when to just print the damn thing out and send it off to its fate."

The goal here is to devise a simple system, something you can follow for every paper to help you root out the embarrassing typos and confusing constructions but also to prevent you from becoming a grammar psycho. Drawing from the advice given in my straight-A interviews, I present in this step a system that meets these criteria. It involves three simple passes through your draft. No more and no less. For those of you who are used to endless editing runs, the idea that three passes is enough might sound suspiciously quick. Or, if you're the kind of person whose idea of proofreading is hitting the spell-check button, multiple runs might seem hopelessly time consuming. But rest assured, the system is efficient and it gets the job done. As we will soon discuss, the key is the specific kind of attention given to each pass. Here is how it works:

The Argument Adjustment Pass

Your first pass through your work should be conducted on your computer. Read carefully, and focus on the presentation of your arguments—don't worry about small grammatical mistakes for the moment. Take in the paper one paragraph at a time. If a section is awkwardly stated, clarify the sentences. If it makes a point you already explained earlier, ruthlessly cut it out. If the argument is lacking detail, add in more sentences as necessary to fully explain your point. If a transition is lacking between topics or paragraphs, add one.

Also be on the lookout for any major structural issues. Sometimes you don't realize until you finish an entire draft that your topic outline wasn't optimal. Don't be afraid to shift around major chunks of text. This is your chance to make serious edits to the structure of your paper, so take this seriously. Do this editing at a time when you are rested and unhurried by upcoming appointments. For a large paper, spread this pass out over several days if possible.

When you're done, your paper may still contain small mistakes. That's okay. You'll fix those next. The goal here is to tweak the argument until you're satisfied that it makes every point that you want to make in the order that you want to make them. Once you're done with this pass, these big picture details are locked in.

The Out Loud Pass

The Argument Adjustment pass is important, but not sufficient by itself. As Robert from Brown explains: "My papers always read differently on the page than on the screen." And as Melanie, a straight-A Dartmouth student, adds: "having a hard copy to read and mark up was absolutely necessary."

Accordingly, for this next pass, you should first print out a copy of your paper, and then take it where you can have some privacy. With a pencil in hand, and this is the important part, begin to read your paper *out loud*. Don't cheat. Use a strong voice and articulate each word as if you're delivering a speech. For a long paper, it may take a long time to read the entire thing, so be prepared to split this into several sessions. You might also want water or hot tea on hand to prevent you from losing your voice. Whatever you do, however, don't avoid actually articulating every word.

Whereas the last pass focused on your arguments, the goal of this pass is to root out small mistakes that might otherwise distract a reader from your engaging thesis. While reading, whenever you come across a grammatical mistake or an awkward construction, mark it clearly on the printout. Then go back up to the beginning of the preceding paragraph and start reading again. After you have marked up the entire document, go back to your computer and enter the changes you noted on your printout. A word of warning—this process always takes longer than expected, so leave yourself plenty of time.

The rationale behind this approach is simple. As Ryan from Dartmouth explains: "Reading it out loud helps you catch typos or strange wording better than reading it in your head." No matter how many times you review a draft, if you're scanning silently, there are certain awkward phrases you might skip over every time—our subconscious minds have a habit of patching over these mistakes when reading our own writing. When you say the words out loud, on the other hand, your ear will catch even minor problems and draw your attention to them. "Something that looks fine on paper will jump out as strange or poorly worded when you hear it," explains Jeremy from Dartmouth. Therefore, by reading the paper out loud, you will catch most mistakes in your paper in just one pass—requiring much less time than the multiple silent reviews necessary to achieve similar results.

The Sanity Pass

Because the previous passes were so careful, you're almost done, and you've only read through your work twice so far! Just to be sure that something embarrassing didn't slip through, it's a good idea to make a final, quick pass through a printed copy of your paper before handing it in. You don't have to do this pass out loud, and feel free to move through it quickly. But definitely use a printed copy, rather than reading on your computer screen, since a hard copy has a better chance of revealing a typo. If possible, separate this pass from the previous two. In fact, it's fine to do this the morning of the deadline. At this point, there should be no major mistakes lurking in your document.

The goal here is twofold. First, as mentioned, this last pass catches stray mistakes. "I tried to always reread my papers before handing them in," explains James, a straight-A student from Dartmouth. "I try to smooth out any last kinks in the flow during that final editing." Second, and perhaps more important, it also provides closure on your paper. Because your work is so polished by this point, this final read-through should essentially go smoothly. As a result, you will develop a better feel for the flow and enjoy the experience of watching your argument unfold. This should help put your mind at ease. After all your work, think of this last pass as your reward. A final review before the paper leaves your hands, probably never to be read by you again. That's why we call it a sanity pass. Once you hand in your paper, you can now confidently tell yourself: "Unless I'm going insane here, I'm pretty sure that I just handed in a damn good piece of writing!"

The Plan in Action

As in Part Two, we end our discussion with a pair of detailed case studies that show you how to put the straight-A system into practice. One focuses on a research paper, whereas the other focuses on a critical analysis essay. Notice how the students in the following case studies adapt the system to the demands of each assignment. And, in both cases, pay attention to how our system reduces the time required for writing, the step most students unfoundedly fear above all others.

Case Study #1—Mindy's Art History Research Paper

Mindy's class on Early American Art doesn't have a final exam. This was, not surprisingly, an important motivation in her decision to register for this particular subject. But now, as the end of the term approaches, Mindy realizes her joy was premature. In place of the final exam, she must instead write a truly intimidating research paper—a thirty- to fifty-page colossus that is worth half of her final grade. The subject matter is wide open; the paper can cover any topic regarding any American artist before the modern period. The professor has made it clear that he expects a large and well-considered argument from each student. He warns the class to start early and work hard. Last-minute efforts will be easily identified and graded with a punitive abandon.

Monday—One Month Before the Due Date

With a month to go until the deadline, Mindy decides it's time to initiate the early stages of the straight-A process. She has no intention of beginning serious researching or writing at this point—it's too early for that; instead, she's simply kicking off the nondemanding "thinking phase" of the paper process: choosing a topic, finding a thesis idea, and then getting a second opinion on the idea from her professor.

For her first step, Mindy spends a half hour Monday night flipping through her class notes, trying to find a topic that piques her interest. Without too much searching, she comes across something promising. Early in the course, when they were studying the American expatriate painter Washington Allston, the professor made a comment about some similarities between Allston's paintings and those of German artist Caspar David Friedrich. The connection was interesting because, as far as the professor knew, the two painters had never met. Mindy had jotted down this comment in her notes along with a little exclamation point. Perhaps this mysterious connection would make for a good topic? Mindy will have to conduct a thesis-hunting expedition to find out for sure, but it's a good start.

Wednesday—Three Weeks and Five Days to the Due Date

Mindy has set aside a couple of hours to lurk in the library and seek out an interesting thesis relating to her topic idea. She starts with the card catalog, and soon finds some monographs that focus entirely on Allston's career. She is able to locate two of these books amid the stacks, and then settles into a nearby study carrel to go through them. For the first hour, she chooses one of the titles, and begins to read it. This helps her build a better understanding of Allston's background and the significance of his career. She realizes, however, that it will be too time consuming for her to continue trying to read the entire book, so she next flips straight to the index. She hits pay dirt in the index of one of the two books: an entry for Caspar David Friedrich. Flipping to that page, she sees a quick one-sentence note about how some author (whose name she doesn't recognize) has posited a connection between Allston and Friedrich. Mindy looks up the reference connected to this sentence and finds the title of an obscure book about philosophy and the early Romantic artists. She finds the call number for this new book, and dives back into the stacks to find it. *Success!* The old manuscript has a chapter devoted to Allston and Friedrich. In fact, it goes so far as to compare two of their paintings and offer an explanation for the similarities.

Mindy makes a photocopy of this chapter and labels it with the information she will need to later cite the book. She leaves the library with her personal copy of this key source in hand.

Friday—Three Weeks and Three Days to the Due Date

Mindy's Art History professor has office hours on Friday afternoons. This is a perfect opportunity for Mindy to seek a second opinion on her thesis idea. The problem, however, is that she doesn't yet have a fully formed idea. For now, she is stuck with only an intriguing topic. With this in mind, she sets aside an hour in the morning to read through her personal copy of the source she found in the library earlier in the week. Her hope is to develop some interesting ideas before office hours that afternoon.

This careful review gives Mindy a better understanding of the author's argument. Fortunately, it's focused. The author looks at a painting by each artist, and he then gives a concise and specific philosophical rationale for both. This focus is fortunate because it leaves a lot of room for Mindy to extend the argument—even though she's not yet sure what this extension will entail. She recognizes that making a well-considered but constrained addition to an already established argument is great way to develop a meaningful but manageable research paper thesis.

During lulls in class that day, Mindy continues to mull over her topic, trying to find a good direction for her thesis. Finally, as the bell rings, an insight hits her. The source she found had explained a shared philosophy between Allston and Friedrich. But it did nothing to explain *why* they both followed this philosophy. If Mindy can find a common source for the artists' shared philosophical interests, then that could make for a fascinating argument!

Arriving at office hours later that afternoon, Mindy explains her thesis idea to her professor. The keyword here is "idea." She does not yet know if this direction will bear fruit. It's possible that her research would turn up no information that helps explain the shared philosophical interests between the two artists, so there is, as is often the case with an engaging thesis idea, an element of risk at this early stage. By meeting with her professor, however, Mindy can greatly reduce this risk. That's a major reason why this step is so important. A professor can draw from his deep pool of knowledge and experience with a topic and generate a reasonable hunch as to whether or not a specific idea seems promising—potentially preventing a frustrating dead end. Fortunately for Mindy, her professor likes the thesis. To him, it seems likely that Mindy can find some evidence for a connection, and he points her toward some well-known Allston and Friedrich monographs that might help her investigation.

Sunday—Three Weeks and One Day to the Due Date

Mindy makes another journey to the library, armed with the book suggestions she received from her professor. Using a well-stocked iPod to abate her boredom, she seeks out two of these books, one for each artist, and makes personal copies of the relevant chapters of each. This takes a good hour to complete, but the work is mindless, so it's not that bad.

Later that evening, Mindy takes these newly acquired personal copies to one of her favorite isolated study spots. She begins to skim through and annotate each. She's not exactly sure what she's looking for, but she knows the more information she has found, copied, and labeled, the better off she will be.

Over time she begins to notice a name that keeps popping up in her Allston book: Samuel Taylor Coleridge, a young European writer and thinker who seemed to have a big impact on Allston.

Mindy hopes to find a mention of Coleridge in the Friedrich material, but she comes up empty-handed. This doesn't dissuade her, however; Friedrich, as it turns out, was hanging around several European philosophical circles at the time. It would not be surprising if there were some sort of connection to Coleridge through one of them.

Her interest piqued, Mindy fires up the library Web page. In class the professor had shown them a journal database that allows you to search for journal articles relating to Art History. Mindy navigates to this page and begins searching, using queries that include both Friedrich and Coleridge. After some sifting through the results, she finds what she is looking for: an article about Friedrich and a group of artists he worked with in Germany. In the abstract for this article, it's mentioned that Coleridge was among the philosophers whose work inspired the group.

A connection has been found! Mindy prints the article and records on the first page all the information she needs to later cite it.

Monday to Sunday—Three Weeks to the Due Date

Excited by her find, Mindy e-mails her professor to explain her newly developed "Coleridge as the missing link" thesis. He loves it and gives her some advice on what sort of additional evidence would help make the case compelling.

With an approved thesis in hand, and a good idea of what additional sources she'll need to form a strong argument, Mindy can now lay out a rough schedule for the steps that follow. Over the next week she will continue to research. Then she will spend the following week crafting her story, building an outline, and getting some final feedback on the argument. This will leave her exactly one week to turn a detailed topic outline into a few dozen pages of coherent writing. The schedule is reasonable in that it doesn't require work every day, and it rarely requires more than a couple hours on any given day—thus the construction of her paper can be easily woven into her already busy schedule.

Following the straight-A approach, Mindy's week of research proceeds mechanically. At each trip to library, on average, Mindy spends one or two hours, during which she finds two or three sources. Each source gets copied, labeled, and annotated. She makes these trips three times during the week and once on Sunday, leaving her with a significant stack of annotated material. Remember, at this point very little thinking has been dedicated to how all of these pieces will fit together into the final paper. That's for the next step.

Monday to Sunday—Two Weeks to the Due Date

Now comes the fun part. In one hand, Mindy has a compelling thesis. In the other hand, she has a stack of annotated personal copies of sources relating to the thesis. Now she has to figure out how to combine the two into a believable story.

There is no mechanical solution to this problem; it requires some serious thinking. And this is exactly what Mindy does. Over the course of this week she takes a lot of walks around campus to consider her argument. She imagines explaining her thesis to an enthralled audience. She revisits her source material often to refresh her memory on what information is available and to stoke the flames of her intellectual curiosity. On a couple of occasions, she even shoehorns her poor roommates into listening to her talk through the current state of her paper idea. By the time Friday rolls around, she has a pretty good idea of how she will present this story. She will start with explaining the philosophical connection between Allston and Friedrich's work (as outlined in that original source she found during her thesis-hunting expedition), explain how this philosophy matches Coleridge's philosophy, and then provide a compelling connection between Coleridge and each of the two artists.

That afternoon, Mindy organizes the personal copies of her sources into three piles, one for each of these three major pieces of her story. She also attends office hours once again. This time she is able to explain to her professor the specifics of her argument and provide examples of the sources she is using to support the argument. He still seems excited about the thesis, and provides some good advice on how to make the argument slightly stronger.

Armed with this knowledge, Mindy spends the weekend constructing her topic-level outline. This takes time, since she has to copy many quotes from her sources and into her outline document. However, she basically did no hard work during the preceding week, other than thinking about her argument whenever she had a free moment, so a little effort over the weekend is not an unreasonable demand.

By Sunday afternoon, Mindy has constructed a thoughtful outline, full of quotes from her sources. She has already discussed her argument with her professor, but before she begins to write, she wants some more opinions. That afternoon, she sets up meetings with two of her classmates to discuss their paper ideas. During both meetings, Mindy is surprised by how little work has been accomplished by her peers—most of them are just starting their search for a thesis—but she does get good feedback on her own argument. Mindy integrates this feedback into her outline, and can now go to sleep confident that the structure of her paper is solid.

Monday to Sunday—*Last Week Before Due Date*

Mindy's plan is to write a little bit each day of the week, with the goal of using the weekend only to edit. Writing, however, takes time. And Mindy's week is busy. Not surprisingly, she doesn't quite meet her goal of finishing an entire rough draft by Friday, but she comes close (when you have a detailed topic-level outline, writing moves much quicker than when you have to continually search through your sources).

That said, this weekend will definitely be a busy one if Mindy is going to get this paper finished and edited in time. Understanding the urgency of the looming deadline, Mindy goes into crisis writing mode on Saturday. Starting early in the morning, Mindy holes herself up in a quiet medical library at the outskirts of campus. Armed with energy boosting snacks and a thermos of coffee, she writes continually, taking short breaks every fifty minutes, until her rough draft is complete. At forty pages long, the paper is both considerable and well thought out.

Nevertheless, Mindy is worried about leaving *all* of the editing until the day before, so after a relaxing dinner she begins her Argument Adjustment Pass on her computer screen. She's tired from a long day of writing, so she makes it through only about a third of the paper before she throws in the towel and goes out to have some fun with her friends for the rest of the night. Getting that little piece of editing done, however, will make her task tomorrow easier to handle.

Sunday morning, Mindy picks up where she left off. By lunchtime she has finished the Argument Adjustment Pass, and now things are starting to look good. After lunch, she hits the gym for an hour to revive her energy and spends some time with a friend to relax and let her mind recharge. Later that afternoon, she brings a printout of her paper to her dorm room and begins her Out Loud Pass. After a break for dinner, she continues this slow but necessary process. By 9 P.M. she finishes the pass. By 10:30 P.M. she has finished integrating the marked changes into her paper. Time for sleep.

Monday—The Due Date

Monday morning, Mindy blocks out one and a half hours to conduct her Sanity Pass. Reading through a printout of the paper rather quickly, she notices a couple of little fixes. More important, however, her confidence in the paper builds. After all the hard work, she is proud of her argument. It's well considered, well supported, and well written. She is excited for her professor to read this.

When class time finally rolls around, Mindy hands in her paper with a smile on her face. She is secretly amused to notice the bleary-eyed stagger with which many of her classmates enter the classroom. For many, this paper came together in a one-week frenzied marathon of simultaneous research and writing. Mindy's work is going to shine compared to these last-minute efforts.

The Result

No surprises here. Mindy's work is a standout. She receives an "A+" and a page full of glowing comments from her professor.

What's important is that Mindy did not spend any more time actually *writing* than her classmates. In fact, her time at the keyboard was probably less than most of her peers because when Mindy sat down in front of the computer, she already knew exactly what to say. Also important, Mindy avoided any painfully long work pushes. Outside of a semi-late night on the day before the due date, and a long day of writing two days before the due date, Mindy avoided ever putting in more than a handful of hours on any given day. Constructing a standout "A" paper hardly interfered with her schedule at all. That's what's so amazing with the straight-A strategy. It improves your grade *and* makes the process seem less time consuming.

Case Study #2—Chris's Film Studies Critical Analysis Essay

After the intense, monthlong effort described in the previous case study, we now move to the opposite end of the paper-writing spectrum. Here we focus on the (comparatively) simple process of writing a short critical analysis essay. Specifically, we consider Chris, whose Film Studies course features a weekly essay assignment. Every Monday, his class watches a film and then is assigned several readings on its merits. The class is then responsible for writing a short (two to five pages) critical analysis essay about the film, describing the student's opinion and how it compares and contrasts to those outlined in the articles read in class that week. The essay is then due the following Monday.

Monday—One Week Before the Due Date

Because these essays are due every week, Chris has discovered, through trial and error, a smart timeline for getting the work done with a minimal impact on his ever-busy schedule. It works as follows:

Monday is for choosing a couple of reading assignments from his syllabus to really read carefully, Tuesday through Thursday is for finishing these readings, Saturday is for outlining, and Sunday is for writing and editing.

On Monday, following his timeline, Chris briefly reviews the syllabus for the week. Usually there are three or four readings assigned, but Christopher has learned that it's usually sufficient to draw from just two sources in his essay. He likes to choose these two in advance so he knows where to focus his attention. After a quick skim of the introductions, he settles on a pair of readings that seem to come to an opposite conclusion about the movie: One loves it, the other hates it. These sorts of stark oppositions tend to provide a lot of meat for a quick analysis.

Tuesday—Six Days Before the Due Date

Chris completes the first reading. It's a chapter from a book and somewhat complicated. He tries to take careful notes on his laptop using the question/evidence/conclusion format described in Part Two. He runs out of time before dinner and ends up having to return to the library later that evening to get the reading done. No big deal.

Wednesday—Five Days Before the Due Date

Chris tackles his second reading. This time he has a good two-hour chunk set aside in the morning, when his energy is high. His progress is steady, and he finishes with time to spare.

Thursday and Friday—Four to Three Days Before the Due Date

Chris doesn't need to think about the essay during these two days. He has more than enough other schoolwork to keep him busy on

Thursday. And Friday, as always, is dedicated to burning off a week of built-up social energy with his friends.

Saturday—Two Days Before the Due Date

During the afternoon, Chris prints out his reading notes. As is his habit, he rereads the notes in his dorm and then takes the long route to the library, thinking about the structure of his essay along the way. He has already decided that he agrees more with the reading assignment that liked the movie. The argument presented in this reading focused mainly on the technical aspects of the film, discussing how the mixture of stark lighting and fast cuts presented a refreshingly modern take on film noir. Chris agrees with these technical arguments, but he also remembers liking the dialogue. At the time, he noted only that it sounded interesting to his ear, but now, in the light of this particular reading, it dawns on him that what made the dialogue so interesting was its mixture of old-style, film-noir catchphrases and a fast, slang-rich, modern street diction. This seems like a cool extension to the argument from the reading, and Chris decides to make this the centerpiece of his essay.

Chris arrives at his favorite study carrel, hidden in a dark corner of the library, pulls out his laptop, and puts together a rough topic outline. He decides to follow a classic format. He will start with a brief summary of the two readings he chose to focus on. He will briefly acknowledge the negative critiques as being, for the most part, true, but then contest that the good qualities of the film outweigh the bad. Here he will flesh out some more details of the positive reading, then add his own extension to this argument by discussing how the dialogue reinforces a similar combination of old and new. A quick conclusion calling the movie an important work will cap the essay nicely. When he's done, the topic skeleton reads as follows:

- Summary of pro and con readings

- Acknowledge and dismiss con reading

- More detailed summary of pro reading

- My argument on the dialogue as modernizing force

- Conclusion

His next step is to copy the relevant quotes from the two assignments into this outline. Because he is dealing with only two sources, each of which he reads carefully, this process doesn't take long.

Finally, even though he has other things to do, Chris holds out for another half hour to write a rough draft of his introduction. For whatever reason, he has found that having some writing done (even if it is only a paragraph) makes it easier to start the next day.

Sunday—One Day Before the Due Date

After sleeping off the effects of a party the night before, Chris returns to the library. As is always the case, Sunday afternoons are for writing, so he knows exactly what to do. Armed with his topic outline, and an already written introduction, this process takes no more than a couple of hours. He heads to an early dinner with a rough draft of the essay complete.

Later that night, Chris completes a quick Argument Adjustment Pass and then prints out a copy to do his Out Loud Pass. Because the essay is only a few pages long, these two passes take no more than an hour. After a TV break, Chris spends fifteen minutes doing a Sanity Pass. And that's it. He's done. He prints out a final draft and jams it in his bag so he won't forget it the next morning.

The Result

Once again, our straight-A student didn't spend any more time reading sources and writing than most of his classmates. But this essay, like his others, will get an A. Why? Because he separated the reading from the thinking and the thinking from the writing. This leads to a well-thought-out argument, clearly articulated. By finishing his reading on Wednesday, Chris had two days for the ideas to float around in the background of his mind. By the time he began thinking about his outline on Saturday, this material had been well digested. By completing a topic-level outline, and then waiting a night before starting to write, Chris had even more time to mull (consciously or not) over his argument in this more polished state. By the time he sat down at his computer on Sunday, the key pieces of this essay had been worked and reworked internally over a long period. This extra attention to the argument came through in his assignment, and, not surprisingly, a high grade followed.

Part Three Cheat Sheet

Step #1. Target a Titillating Topic

- Start looking for an interesting topic early.

Step #2. Conduct a Thesis-Hunting Expedition

- Start with general sources and then follow references to find the more targeted sources where good thesis ideas often hide.

Step #3. Seek a Second Opinion

- A thesis is not a thesis until a professor has approved it.

Step #4. Research like a Machine

- Find sources.

- Make personal copies of all sources.

- Annotate the material.

- Decide if you're done. (If the answer is "no," loop back to #1.)

Step #5. Craft a Powerful Story

- There is no shortcut to developing a well-balanced and easy-to-follow argument.

- Dedicate a good deal of thought over time to getting it right.

- Describe your argument in a topic-level outline.

- Type supporting quotes from sources directly into your outline.

Step #6. Consult Your Expert Panel

- Before starting to write, get some opinions on the organization of your argument and your support from classmates and friends who are familiar with the general area of study.

- The more important the paper, the more people who should review it.

Step #7. Write Without the Agony

- Follow your outline and articulate your points clearly.

- Write no more than three to five pages per weekday and five to eight pages per weekend day.

Step #8. Fix, Don't Fixate

- Solid editing requires only three careful passes:

  - *The Argument Adjustment Pass*: Read the paper carefully on your computer to make sure your argument is clear, fix obvious errors, and rewrite where the flow needs improvement.

  - *The Out Loud Pass*: Carefully read out loud a printed copy of your paper, marking any awkward passages or unclear explanations.

  - *The Sanity Pass*: A final pass over a printed version of the paper to check the overall flow and to root out any remaining errors.

Conclusion

"All the people I ever admired
and respected led balanced lives—
studying hard, partying hard, as well as
being involved in activities and getting
a decent amount of sleep each night.
I really think this is the only logically
defensible way of doing things."

Chris, *a straight-A college student*

Congratulations! You're about to embark on a new and exciting chapter in your college experience. It doesn't matter if you agree with every piece of advice you just encountered; what's important is that by making it this far, you've learned two crucial insights: (1) Brute force study habits are incredibly inefficient; and (2) It is possible to come up with techniques that work much better and require much less time. With this in mind, you are now prepared to leap past the majority of your classmates and begin scoring top grades without sacrificing your health, happiness, or social life.

I leave you, however, with one last request. Once you put these ideas into practice and begin to experience their many benefits, remember what your academic life was like before your transformation. Then, the next time you see a poor student huddled in the library, bleary-eyed after an all-nighter, or encounter a friend near a nervous breakdown from the sheer stress of looming deadlines, take him aside and let him know that it doesn't have to be this way. Tell him that studying doesn't just mean reading and rereading your notes and assignments as many times as possible; nor does paper writing necessitate all-night marathons at the keyboard. These tasks don't have to be so draining. They don't have to be something you fear. With the right guidance, a willingness to eschew conventional wisdom, and a little experimentation, academics can be transformed into one of the most satisfying and fulfilling components of your college experience. You know this now. Share your knowledge.

As our generation finds itself increasingly stressed and disillusioned with life paths that we feel have been imposed upon us from the outside, this lesson takes on a particular importance. By mastering the skills in this book you are, in effect, taking control of your own young life. You are declaring to the world that you're not at college just because it seemed like the thing to do; instead, you're there to master new areas of knowledge, expand your mental abilities, and have some fun in the process. You're also denying your major or the climate of the job market the right to dictate what you can or can't do after graduation. By scoring exceptional grades, you are opening the door to many interesting and competitive opportunities that allow you, and not anyone else, to make the decision of what post-college pursuits will bring you the most fulfillment. In the end, therefore, this book is about so much more than just grades; it is about taking responsibility for your own journey through life. I wish you the best of luck in this adventure, and hope this advice helps you to launch an exciting future.

Acknowledgments

I would like to thank the following straight-A students for taking the time to discuss with me the details of their study habits. Their responses were well considered and insightful. I hope they remain as excited as I am to spread their wisdom to a new generation of motivated students.

Jason Auerbach, Lacey J. Benson, Robert Blair, Christopher R. Bornhorst, Wendy Brill, Melanie Chiu, Nathalie Cohen, John Corwin, Christine DeLucia, Hrishikesh Desai, Nic Duquette, Ryan A. Foley, Chris Goodmacher, Lee Hochbaum, Doris Huang, Andrew Huddleston, Sean Kass, Suzanne Kim, Chien Wen Kun, Worasom Kundhikanjana, Rachel Lauter, Frank Lehman, Simon McEntire, Vito Menza, Greta S. Milligan, Rielle Navitski, Tyra A. Olstad, Anna S. Parachkevova, David R. Peranteau, David Philips, Jeremy S. Presser, Jonathan Sar, Imran Sharih, Gaurav Singhania, Laura M. Smalligan, Lydia J. Smith, Suzanne Smith, Jenna Steinhauer, Lukasz Strozek, Matthew Swetnam, James F. Tomczyk, Leigh C. Vicens, Srigowri Vijayakumar, John P. Welsh II, and Gretchen Ziegler.

In addition, this work would not have been possible without the tireless efforts of my agent, Laurie Abkemeier, and my editor, Ann Campbell, both of whom put up with my ever-evolving and increasingly emphatic theories on the personality, hopes, and dreams of the modern college student and always steered me back to the core work of uncovering meaningful advice and expressing it clearly. I must also thank Julie, my partner and muse. Without her unwavering support and patience, this project would not have been possible.

About the Author

Cal Newport graduated from Dartmouth College, earned a Ph.D. from MIT, and is now an associate professor of computer science at Georgetown University. The author of multiple bestselling books, he runs the popular blog *Study Hacks*, which explores the impact of technology on our ability to perform productive work and lead satisfying lives. His contrarian ideas have been featured on many major media platforms, including the *New York Times, Wall Street Journal, Washington Post, The Economist,* and NPR. Visit him online at calnewport.com.

Don't miss Cal Newport's other popular student success guides.

"This book is the perfect high school graduation gift. . . . Highly recommended because it is full of practical tips that will help high school grads take the next step in life."
—*Money*

"As a former Ivy League admissions officer, I was overjoyed to see a book that hit the nail on the head regarding selective college admissions and how to take the process in stride. Students will find his book extremely useful and admissions officers will be relieved to see applicants who escape the cookie-cutter syndrome."
—Dr. Michele Hernández, author of *A Is for Admission* and cofounder of Top Tier Admissions

Available wherever books are sold